Opera Coaching

Opera Coaching

Professional Techniques and Considerations

Alan Montgomery

Routledge
Taylor & Francis Group
New York   London

Published in 2006 by
Routledge
Taylor & Francis Group
270 Madison Avenue
New York, NY 10016

Published in Great Britain by
Routledge
Taylor & Francis Group
2 Park Square
Milton Park, Abingdon
Oxon OX14 4RN

Printed in the United States of America on acid-free paper
10 9 8 7 6 5 4 3 2 1

International Standard Book Number-10: 0-415-97601-4 (Softcover) 0-415-97600-6 (Hardcover)
International Standard Book Number-13: 978-0-415-97601-5 (Softcover) 978-0-415-97600-6 (Hardcover)
Library of Congress Card Number 2005030679

Library of Congress Cataloging-in-Publication Data

Montgomery, Alan, 1946-
    Opera coaching : professional techniques and considerations / Alan Montgomery.
        p. cm.
    Includes bibliographical references (p.) and index.
    ISBN 0-415-97600-6 (hardback) -- ISBN 0-415-97601-4 (pbk.) 1. Opera coaching. I. Title.

MT956.M66 2006
782.1'14071--dc22

2005030679

Taylor & Francis Group
is the Academic Division of Informa plc.

Visit the Taylor & Francis Web site at
http://www.taylorandfrancis.com

and the Routledge Web site at
http://www.routledge-ny.com

CONTENTS

PREFACE

The trained pianist can make a good living and have a respectable career in many areas. One professional field many pianists overlook, however, is that of coaching. Some musicians have no idea what a coach does. The definition is simple and yet extremely wide-ranging. A coach helps musicians learn music, although the help is not usually of a technical nature. That work is reserved for the vocal or instrumental teacher. The coach leads the musician being coached to consider such things as articulation, phrasing, tempo, intonation, stylistic concerns, dynamics, and even the overall shape of a piece.

These issues can pose complex challenges for the young musician, even in so-called "pure" music — that music which has no text or dramatic program. A violinist, for instance, must find the musical path to performing a four-movement sonata. This means developing not only the technique needed to perform the work; it also means discovering where the climaxes and low points might really be. Music ebbs and flows, even when the tempo is relatively constant. Coaching a singer instead of an instrumentalist presents several significant additional problems not found in coaching instrumental literature. Some instrumentalists like to say that there are "musicians" and there are "singers." In truth there are instrumentalists and there are singers, and the presence or absence of musical talent can be just as pronounced in one as the other. The added challenges of being a singer sometime make those singers seem less musical than their instrumentalist counterparts.

A singer is his or her own instrument, and he or she can never be away from it. Emotion, which must flow into every phrase they sing, must not affect their ability to produce their voices. They must also perform almost everything they sing by memory. This can be a great challenge, particularly with the music of the twentieth century or when the opera being performed stretches to several hours. Acting skills must also enter into the equation, even if the singer is choosing the recital stage as his or her primary performance venue. Few consider, too, that singing is the only profession in which a person must act and react in two or three languages not his or her own. Virgil Thomson was once quoted as saying, "Opera singers should never act." The full quote, of course, goes on to say that they should "react" instead.[1] Each nationality may think that singing in a foreign language is primarily the problem of that country and that others do not face these challenges. But only singers from France, Germany, and Italy have a sufficiently wide range of repertoire that they can have a career singing in only their native language, and most of them sing numerous roles outside their language. It is just not an acceptable practice for a singer to stand and sing by rote syllables and tones with no understanding of what he or she is singing.

It is the job of the coach to help singers learn their roles in all aspects possible. This means that a coach must deal with languages, musical problems that arise, dramatic and vocal concerns a singer may have, play for rehearsals — musical and staging — and be able to do a multitude of peripheral duties, such as conduct backstage, play chimes or other assorted instruments, and orchestrate *banda* sections when necessary. (I've even been a guest screamer for the tenor in *Tosca*.)

As with the singer, a vocal coach must have a firm knowledge of the basic languages used in Western vocal music: English, French, German, and Italian. Other languages have entered the repertoire recently as well: Russian, Czechoslovakian, Spanish, Hungarian, and even Finnish. This must go beyond simple word-for-word translating. It must include understanding the implications of certain texts, both the sociopolitical for the compositional time (or for our own time), and for the development of a character. The coach, who has delved into various areas of vocal composition and theatrical experiences, will find that work an invaluable asset to the singer trying to learn his or her first role. Some understanding of singing (even if the coach has little real voice) is also frequently quite useful.

A simple example will suffice to demonstrate what is meant in the above paragraph. In *Turandot* by Giacomo Puccini, when Liù sings "Tu che di gel sei cinta" ("You who of ice are girded") she addresses Turandot as "Tu." How dare a slave girl address a Princess in the informal "Tu!" But at that moment, with that one word, Liù strips aside all rank and speaks to Turandot woman to woman. She has nothing to lose, because she knows suicide is her only option.

The difficulties of breaking into the singing business compound the problems of being a singer. The business of singing requires determination to fight against rather tall odds and selling one's own talent and self on a daily basis. It also requires considerable knowledge. Through careful study of singers from earlier generations, a singer can learn the kind of voice appropriate to a given repertoire. Today many young singers consider the thought that they should familiarize themselves with these earlier singers to be ludicrous. Yet some famous and very knowledgeable singers have learned reams from recordings of people, who recorded as far back as the dawn of recording itself. Among other things, these recordings may actually show the original artists, thus presenting as closely as possible the thoughts of the composer (who may, in fact, be accompanying on the recording). It is astonishing how much other disciplines know about their work area and how little many singers know or care.

The pianist who ventures into coaching singers must also have a wide knowledge of both singers and repertoire. This is not only because a singer may arrive, with no advance notice at all, expecting to be helped in standard (and plenty of nonstandard) repertoire. That same singer may justifiably ask for advice concerning certain roles or repertoire choices. The coach who has a strong understanding of voices and of what is "usual" in a particular piece of music can help far more than one who has little idea of such things.

The guidance behind the successful singer is one of the various areas of music that has suffered a great deal of late. Many famous singers have lauded conductors and coaches for the guidance they were given. And many also bemoan the fact that good vocal coaches and conductors (those who really know and understand voices and repertoire) are becoming harder and harder to find. This volume will deal with many of the problems facing a coach. It should help the pianist interested in this field find ways to open the door to a rewarding and lengthy career. Such a career requires little musical memory work and few performance opportunities (unless accompanying assignments come along as well). It might even require the coach to play harpsichord in performances of Mozart and Rossini operas. It *does* at times require imagination, learning to follow a conductor, and long hours in rehearsals — all of these with seemingly limitless reserves of strength and good humor.

ACKNOWLEDGMENTS AND DEDICATION

I want to give thanks to many friends who have given me encourage-ment in the writing of this volume. Most particularly, I wish to thank Dr. Victoria Vaughan, whose chapter on the stage manager's perspec-tive is quite important. It was her suggestions that led to the many hours I have spent writing and rewriting the text. I also wish to give special thanks to Andrew Bertoni, whose skill with computers enabled him to write out for me the various musical examples appearing within the text. My colleague, Daniel Michalak, has also given major support and ideas toward the thoughts I have put forth here.

I would be remiss if I did not thank Judith Layng, Steven Daigle, Victoria Vaughan, and Jonathon Field, the stage directors with whom I have worked most frequently. They have given me a solid perspective on the connection of music and text. Robert Baustian, Robert Spano, Michel Singher, Paul Polivnick, Stephen Lord, and many other con-ductors have also given me major encouragement along the way in my coaching career. The late Tibor Kozma and Wolfgang Vacano taught me much about both conducting and about coaching. Their care with the shaping of music shows itself in many of the chapters of this book.

This book is dedicated to all of these people, but most particularly to my mother. She did not always understand what an opera coach does any better than many other people do, but she always supported my efforts, and for that I cannot give her enough thanks and love.

1

Techniques

This portion covers the basic techniques needed to coach soloists and ensembles and accompany rehearsals.

1

KNOWING THE SCORE

THE LATE CONDUCTOR TIBOR KOZMA used to invoke the wrath of God on poor conducting students by accusing them of breaking the eleventh commandment: *Thou shalt know thy score.* With him it was not just a matter of generally knowing the right notes. He expected the conductor to know the notes completely, and he wanted that same conductor to understand the implication in shape and color of every note in the score. In other words, the conducting student needed to know not only the black and white of the score, but also the gray. This does not mean that he wanted every conductor to conduct scores from memory. He deplored that practice. But one had to know a score so well that one could. Having the score in front of you means that you can correct a mistake that appears suddenly but which has never happened in rehearsal.

The black and white of a score means simply knowing everything that is printed in the score from the first measure to the end. If the dynamics, phrasing, tempi, or basic shape is wrong, then the conductor does not know the score. But the gray area includes the intangibles: knowledge of stylistic concerns and traditions associated with a given piece. They are just as important to the knowledge of the score as the black-and-white notes found on the page. Coaches, even if they play almost exclusively from piano-vocal scores, need to be able to study the orchestral scores, improving those vocal scores with notations from the knowledge learned in the fuller score. This may also mean learning which editions of scores to trust and which ones to avoid.

3

1. THE BLACK AND WHITE

Around 1940, new editions began appearing that made a conscientious effort to correct the mistakes printed in earlier editions. The mammoth Mussorgsky edition, published by the State Publishing House in Moscow, was one of the first. Although it was left incomplete, it nonetheless made many people realize what mistakes had crept into prior editions. It also showed clearly the changes that had been made by well-meaning hands in many of Mussorgsky's scores. These critical editions showed us that, over the years, copyists had managed to omit or move critically important markings in the manuscripts. These include accidentals (sharps or flats), phrase markings, bowings, and even entire measures. The "critical editions" of the music of Mussorgsky and other composers try to correct these mistakes and omissions. Occasionally errors still occur, but for the most part the problems have been greatly minimized. Even standard repertoire works such as *La Bohème* or *L'Elisir d'amore* exist in critical editions. Their popularity may in fact have engendered more mistakes due to the repeated need for copyists. These editions are not ends in and of themselves, but they are a wonderful aid in reaching the most expressive (and correct) renditions of a composer's ideas. These editions include orchestral and piano-vocal scores of operas, and they exist for instrumental music as well. They even include alternate passages where a composer may have changed his mind. Now libraries are shelving the "critical editions" of complete works of Mozart, Rossini, Verdi, Johann Strauss Jr., and others.

Some coaches are able to play from orchestral scores. Most coaches do not. In addition to the difficulty such an exercise creates, there are many more page turns. Many coaches choose to concentrate on learning piano-vocal scores. A few operas can be played relatively easily from full score, most particularly those from the Baroque era. In fact, since the compositions consist basically of a violin and continuo line, some people choose the full score for those works. But once beyond a work from the classical era, say, *Don Giovanni*, most coaches will gladly resort to the reductions.

This does not mean, however, that a coach should avoid looking through the orchestral score. One can learn many things from such a study. In Verdi's *Falstaff*, the last page of the vocal score of act 1, scene 1 contains many sixteenth notes. They seem to be boiling away, reflecting Falstaff's fury at his comrades' chaste "honor." As he is chasing them as well, it would seem to be a good reduction of what the orchestra plays. But even a cursory look into the score (or a decent listen to any recording) will show that above the churning violins, a trumpet

Figure 1   (a) Verdi — *Falstaff M* — Act One, scene 1 Closing (excerpt — right hand only as usually printed); (b) *Falstaff M* — Act One, scene 1 Closing (excerpt — as one should play it).

line is dominating the texture, blaring out a rhythmic variant of the "L'onore!" theme. A coach needs to write this into the score and play *it* instead of all of those violin figures. (See Figure 1a and Figure 1b.)

Another example might be found in the aria "Non più andrai" from Mozart's *Le Nozze di Figaro*. On the last page of the aria, most reductions give the alternating figure of a triplet in unison. But against this is a wonderfully military rhythm in the tympani. This can easily be inserted and played simultaneously with the triplets. (See Figure 2.)

Coaches may benefit in other ways from perusing scores. In addition to these types of figures, which can be added and played, one can make corrections of vocal rhythms, dynamics, and even text. The more a coach knows about good editions, the better. Some editions are excellent although expensive. Others are equally good, but their price does not necessarily reflect that. Dover editions of Mozart opera orchestral scores are reprints of the Peters publication edited by Georg

Figure 2   Mozart — *Le Nozze di Figaro* — "Non più andrai" — excerpt from the close of the aria.

Schünemann and Kurt Soldan and are quite decent. Some editions, even some that cost a great deal, cannot be trusted. Even the best editions have some mistakes now and then. One reason for this might be a firm printing an opera in a language not its own. The engravers make errors in the language simply because they don't know it innately. There are also operas in which early editions have rhythms and words different from newer ones, and questions arise as to the correct reading — and recordings, even those conducted by the composer, don't always answer the questions sufficiently.

Two examples are found in *Le Nozze di Figaro*. The first occurs when Figaro is singing "Non più andrai," his closing aria of act 1. The Neue Mozart Ausgabe (NMA) as published by Bärenreiter gives Figaro the following syllabification:

> "con le ne-vi e i sol-i-o-ni, al con-cer-to . . ." with "vi e i" all on one note.

Correct would be:

> "con le ne-vi ei sol-io-ni, al con-cer-to . . ." with "e i" occupying the next note after "vi" and "solioni" being a three- not four-syllable word.

Second, when Antonio bursts through the door in the act 2 finale, he complains that someone has jumped down from the window onto his flowers. The translation for the flowers is usually "geraniums." The original is "garofani," which refers to a small pink flower indigenous to Italy. The critical editions (including the Peters/Dover above) accent this as "ga-ro-FA-ni," following the usual Italian rule of accenting the next to the last syllable. Unfortunately, the correct accent is "ga-RO-fa-ni." This may be Mozart's mistake or a simple printer's error. Even if it is Mozart's mistake, an editor should correct it (possibly footnoting the discrepancy). A later recitative accents the word correctly.

Of course, some composers set words oddly, leaning into wrong accents. Sometimes this can be on purpose, a quirk of a composer to give a passage unusual lift and distinction. Bizet's *Carmen* is a case in point, with many unusual accents that seem wrong but which lift the ordinary to the inspired. In Stravinsky's *The Rake's Progress*, the composer shows an occasional uncertainty with English. Handel's setting of the text for *Messiah* is frequently altered in performance to erase some critical errors in syntax and accent, brought on by his lack of correct speaking ability in English. Thus his setting of "If God be for *us*, who can be *against* us" is usually altered to "If God be *for* us, who can be *against* us." The syntax is then correct.

Other mistakes come about when Italian composers elide syllables together. Some editions make inaccurate divisions of these elisions, and improper accents result. (The above-mentioned excerpt from "Non più andrai" is a case in point.) For this reason, a coach must really understand the languages. He or she may just be called upon to correct the text underlay in any given place. (A cursory look at some original manuscripts will make quite clear how some of these errors get started.)

Learning to play a score usually means also learning to sing a score. As painful as this may be for some coaches (and those listening to them), the reasons are clear. When a coach can sing a score, the knowledge of the score and the text is much greater. Then a singer's mistake will jump out at the coach, because it is not what he or she has learned to sing. Besides, a coach will have to throw cues to the singer throughout the coaching sessions. Learning the text and delivering it in coachings (with nuances and colors appropriate for the real singer) can make many shadings of text clear, and it is a wonderful way to explore the meanings of the texts and to let the nuances jump out. The singer being coached can learn to react to a line far more naturally if that line is delivered with the intended meaning, whether lighthearted or menacing.

I have found that just because recordings all do some phrases the same way does not necessarily mean those recordings are all correct. A careful study of even the most hackneyed and familiar aria, such as "La donna è mobile" in *Rigoletto*, will reveal many markings that are almost universally ignored. Grouping of phrases may also make more sense in some way different than the traditional phrasing might indicate. Of course, in order to study the correct markings, one must find scores that are correctly marked. If a marking seems really odd — a phrase carried over where it makes no sense — it bears searching out other editions. Even critical editions of scores might be wrong. The joy in such searching is in the discoveries, not in the work at finding those revelations. If a photocopy of the original manuscript is available, that is always best.

Frequently the score will also contain printed mistakes that need to be corrected. In Georges Bizet's *Carmen*, the card scene is usually printed with the solo lines for Frasquita and Mercedes reversed. Many conductors want the corrections made, but some do not. The Oeser edition, though controversial in many ways, gets those parts absolutely correct. In Micaëla's aria, "Je dis," the middle section contains an unusual hiccup on the words "ar-*ti*-FI-ce maudit." Bizet wrote an even rhythm, placing the correctly accented syllable on an unaccented note rhythmically, but making it the highest note. He knew that the French can sing against an obvious accent with wonderful results. Someone along the way felt the need to accent the "obvious" syllable and changed the rhythm to the hiccup. It should be sung evenly, as Bizet wrote it. (A similar dislocation of the usual accent can be found in the Seguidilla at the words "mon brigadier.")

If a language has some exceptions to the rules, it is a good idea, when preparing a score, to indicate them. Even experts cannot always remember the exceptions. Underline the *s* that is occasionally sounded in French, since it is not usually sounded.[1] Write phonetically what should be sung, if it flies in the face of a normal reading. Names give particular problems. One must decide whether to pronounce them in the fashion of the language being sung or in the manner of the names' origin. Is it Butterfly (*Buhterfly*), as in English, or is it Butterfly (*Booterfly*), as in Italian? Argument may even occur over the correct pronunciation of a word. "Così" is pronounced with either a *z* or an *s* sound in the middle, depending on what part of Italy you use for reference.

Learning the printed score should start with a pianistic work-through of a score. Some scores have movements of great difficulty. Others are simpler, requiring only a little working out. The vocal score for Stravinsky's *The Rake's Progress* needs a good bit of rewriting to make the score playable by even the most talented players. The reason is not just that it is difficult music to play, but that it is frequently written in an awkward fashion, with hand crossings, octave displacements, and rhythmic difficulties — all of which must be delivered with a musically convincing rendition. Some of these awkward moments can be alleviated with minor rewriting. A glance at the accompaniment to the outburst of Baba the Turk in act 2 will make this point very clear.

Performances include the difficult harpsichord part, usually played by a coach. The "Graveyard Scene" gains its whole aura through this instrument, and, in this scene, it is quite difficult to play. (Harpsichord and piano playing in the pit is an example of performing duties coaches must assume. These can be rewarding but also quite difficult.)

The basket scene from *Falstaff* will also take a great deal of work for the pianist to endure playing all of the way through the scene in staging rehearsals. In addition to the sheer difficulty of playing the orchestral reduction, the vocal parts enter at such a furious pace that the singers need considerable ensemble rehearsals to get the scene right. Staging rehearsals take many repetitions to get everything blocked and staged. All of these require the coach to endure multiple traversals of the scene. The stamina required can make a three-hour rehearsal seem twice that!

Learning to sing and play the score may also mean marking some ideas about interpretations into the score. An example comes in the last act of Puccini's *Tosca*. I've always felt (and Placido Domingo, in *My Operatic Roles*, wrote in "agreement"[2]) that Cavaradossi is just as ecstatic about being set free as Tosca is in telling him. We hear only one brief reference to his political savvy. Tosca says that Scarpia has signed the papers for their escape.

> Cavaradossi: "La prima sua grazia è questa … This is the first time he has been so gracious."

> Tosca: "E l'ultima … And the last."

After the greater part of the ecstatic duet, Tosca "happens" to mention that their freedom must be preceded by a mock execution. Cavaradossi realizes immediately that Tosca has been duped. His vocal line becomes monochromatic, even, and uninflected. He knows that the execution will not be fake but real. This adds greater poignancy to his "Parlami ancor come dolci …" ("Tell me again how sweet …"). A coach must find these points and present them to a singer. Even if the director does not see things this way, the singer may have added insights. They may not use everything in production A, but production B three years later may bring in these other shadings.

A singer may sing roles many times and yet be asked to change basic conceptions in a new production. One such singer might come to a production ready to deliver his "usual" rendition, but a director may challenge him with new ideas. In "Se vuol ballare," Figaro might be a swaggering and boastful servant in one production, a seething servant emotionally wounded by his best friend in the next. Taken at a true minuet tempo, it may not be about stylish posturing, but it may become instead about an ego recovering its balance. Even if the singer vows to himself never to do it that way again, such ideas will color aspects of the next productions, too.

In coachings and stagings, a coach can resort to anything plausible at the piano to reproduce the score with flair. The coach may sometimes sing lines that hands cannot cover. Finding many of those added notes, octave doublings, and mistakes to make the score far clearer will also make it more difficult to play. But they make the sound coming from a piano much closer to what the singer will hear.

Reductions from an orchestral score can produce some of those mistakes. Copyists, reducing from full score to piano-vocal score, sometimes make inadvertent slips in transposition or reading of clefs. This can result in some odd harmonies. On the other hand, omission of some notes can lead to a false sense of harmony. In the fourth act finale of *Le Nozze di Figaro*, the Count's climactic "No — no, no, no, no, no" is accompanied with strings in unison. But on the last note, given in some piano editions as another unison, there is actually a very prominent second in the horns. It is the crashing dissonance of the Count's brutality, and it also points ahead to his undoing.

Playing (and singing) a score has its own difficulties. Scores like Berg's *Wozzeck* or *Lulu* increase these difficulties. They simply have too many notes to cover with two hands. The Richards, Wagner and Strauss, wrote scores that are equally difficult. It becomes necessary to find ways to play the *melos* (the essential chords and melodic patterns) and leave some of the fancier passagework on the page unplayed. As wonderful as it might be to hear every note, a piece like "The Ride of the Valkyries" requires some judicious faking to play it at one piano. The harder moments of these operas will require marking what needs to be played and what doesn't. A highlighter is a great friend at such times. Like that page in *Falstaff*, you sometimes need to know what the singer needs to hear. Play that, and let the smaller filigree recede in importance. The singer is hanging on the harmonic progressions and melodic kernels that jump out. Examples of the simplification process will appear in the chapter on Wagner and Strauss.

In the third act finale to Smetana's *The Bartered Bride*, the music moves quite quickly. When everyone is singing, Smetana takes the tonality from F major into a momentary D♭ major. Rather than play every note correctly (and that is quite a feat in itself), the able coach should make the harmonic shifts more prevalent, so the singers can hear what they need to hear. (See Figure 3.) (This score also exists in editions that are in need of considerable editorial corrections. Vocal lines have been adjusted from Czech to German and then to English, with many specifics of Smetana's writing having been lost along the way.)

Reductions aren't infallible. I have long found that the piano-vocal score for "Una furtiva lagrima" from *L'Elisir d'amore* by Donizetti needs adjusting. The opening passage as printed sounds like a "Ständchen" by Brahms, pretty but rather ponderous. The left hand is printed an octave too low. It is a harp playing in the same register in which it will play during the sung portion of the aria (printed correctly in Figure 4). Despite the bassoon line sounding some of the same pitches

Figure 3   Smetana — *The Bartered Bride* — Act Three — simplification of accompaniment (with the vocal lines shown only partially).

simultaneously with the harp line, it takes only a little practice, and the appropriate effect can be achieved.

A passage like the opening of act 3 of Richard Strauss's *Der Rosenkavalier* or the turbulent orchestral outburst that leads into Vanessa's aria "Do not utter a word, Anatol" (from Samuel Barber's *Vanessa*) are filled with cross-rhythms and intricate counterpoint, all of which a pianist might want to play. But a coach must decide what is most important

Figure 4   Donizetti — *L'Elisir d'Amore* — "Una furtiva lagrima" — Introduction shown as it should be played.

and find ways to play that, eliminating the rest. In the *Rosenkavalier* excerpt, this means finding a way to play both the pit music and the backstage waltz, since a stage director will use sounds from both for specific actions. Here listening to a recording might give a good indication of what the *melos* really is.

The Barber excerpt also includes backstage sounds. While the sleigh bells are not absolutely necessary, the rhythm of the earlier bell (before "Must the winter come so soon?") is quite important and helps the singer know rhythmically where she is. (The coach may be called upon to conduct these backstage sounds, too.)

This covers some idea of the black-and-white study of a score. Playing a score at a piano is by definition an approximation of the orchestral fabric. A good pianist can make a piano sound differently depending on what kind of instrument plays a given line. The coach should know if a line is played by an oboe or the first violins, horns or violas. Even in Beethoven's "Les Adieux" sonata, the opening is definitely reminiscent of horn writing in any number of symphonies. The pianist could (should?) play the piece with a rounder tone, imitating a horn's tone.[3]

2. LEARNING THE GRAY

The gray substance associated with a score is far more difficult to learn. It involves absorbing style, tradition, and different demands of historically informed performances. It also necessitates understanding the differences of vocal production and ornamentation in all styles from Monteverdi to Britten and Glass. It's a very tall order, but one, perhaps, not quite as impossible as expected.

In the late 1930s Luigi Ricci published, through G. Ricordi, a series of three books entitled *Variazioni–Cadenze–Tradizioni*. These books are divided into *voci femminili, voci maschili,* and *voci miste*: one book for women, one for men, and one for mixed voices (more arias, and duets).[4] The attempt was to put in print variations (embellishments), standard cadenzas, and traditions (cuts and tempo modifications), which Italian opera had accrued up to that time. Ricci covered only the standard repertoire in Italy of that era. Today some of that literature has faded away, and certainly more has resurfaced. But the important things these books give are the principles. If you understand these carefully studied variations from the written text, you can understand how they were made, and then making decisions of your own is not so difficult. The volumes are actually fairly comprehensive. Estelle Liebling also gathered traditional cadenzas (adding some new ones, too) for coloratura soprano.[5]

Of course, historically singers would have made their own changes. Until recordings became the norm and every embellishment was impressed in vinyl, singers devised their own ornaments, tailoring them to their own voices. Some became quite the norm, but others were different for each singer. Now everyone tries to sing the same thing, whether it fits his or her voice or not. And worse, the audience expects the same changes, because they too have heard the recordings. A revelatory exercise is to take various recordings of the tenor aria "Ah si, ben mio" from Verdi's *Il Trovatore*, starting with the recitative directly preceding it. Begin the collection with Caruso and progress with as many examples as can be found up through Domingo, Pavarotti, and Alagna. It is possible to use recordings not in Italian, too. The differences in the arias won't be so eye-opening, but the recitatives are all quite different one from the other. Yet, if you do a similar thing with "Una furtiva lagrima" from Donizetti's *L'Elisir d'amore*, you will find the tenors all taking almost exactly the same cadenza at the end, differing only in which words they use for the last V–I cadence.

Sopranos singing "Regnava nel silenzio" from Donizetti's *Lucia di Lammermoor* will sing some cadenzas differently, adding high notes here and there as they see fit, but the major embellishments of the second verse of the cabaletta will almost all be exactly the same. Baritones singing the famous aria "Bella siccome un angelo" from Donizetti's *Don Pasquale* will also use the same alteration of the final cadenza, despite Ricci listing several other possibilities, and they will almost all avoid many specific markings Donizetti made such as portamento, staccato, and so on.

Another gray area coaches must understand is the tradition of cutting music. Composers like Verdi and Donizetti followed certain strict forms. These were strict both in formal outlines and in the poetic scansion required. Today, though we sometimes acknowledge the strength of those original forms, we see the many reasons for shortening the operas. The first reason is the sheer length of some roles. Violetta is quite a trial for even the most technically secure singer. Performed uncut, each aria has two verses, and the duets have sections that are almost never performed today outside of recordings. For "Ah, fors'è lui" and "Addio del passato" to be given with both verses intact is very tiring. Add to that the complete duets from act one with Alfredo and from act 2 with Germont, and then the complete version of "Parigi, o cara," and you have a strenuous role.

Similarly, the tenor role in *La Traviata* is taxing for a lyric tenor. Adding his act 2 cabaletta, "O mio rimorso, infamia," lifts the role into spinto (dramatic) tenor territory, eliminating some otherwise very good Alfredos. The lyric tenor just cannot summon that much vocal power. This cabaletta is frequently cut altogether, but even those tenors who insist on singing it usually reduce it to one verse. It is only slightly lighter than the tenor aria Verdi had written two months earlier, "Di quella pira," from *Il Trovatore*, also in C major.

Cutting goes beyond just second stanzas. Duet cuts abound in the Italian repertoire. Some cuts, amounting to only two or four measures, seem ludicrous but are sometimes made to make passagework easier, and ensembles, such as that one which closes act 2 of *Lucia di Lammermoor*, are so seldom given complete that opera house choruses would have to do major restudy of the choruses if those cuts were opened. A coach needs to know these traditions, knowing the principle of the cuts if not the actual cuts themselves. Cutting may involve the singer staying quiet while the orchestra plays two or more measures. This allows the singer to catch a needed breath and swallow, usually before the last (unwritten) high note.

Very few printed scores print the optional cuts. What is usually done is that one finds a passage that seems to go on too long. One finds a place near the beginning where the cut can begin, then finds the ending passage. Of course, the keys must match, and the leap must make sense in all vocal parts, though even that can sometimes be written around by resolving a voice into the measure following the cut. The best ways physically to cut are these: At the beginning of the cut, make a line through the entire system (possibly curving around a necessary extra note of resolution), with a bracket seeming to bar off the cut music like this:

[

Above this write the letters: VI–. After the cut, write a similar mark as:

]

Above this write the letters: –DE. If the cut is from one part of a page to later on the same page or the facing page, a single, dark line can be drawn from the first bracket to the next, allowing the coach's eye to follow the line from the beginning to the end of the cut easily. If the cut involves several pages, it is helpful to put a marking such as the following:

[VI– 163 / 3 / 5

This means that you cut to page 163, system 3, measure 5. When indicating the measure, it almost invariably means the beginning of the measure, not the end of it. After the cut it is seldom necessary to write where the cut came from, since that is not the direction one reads a score. Paper clips also help to facilitate making such cuts without making them permanent.

This system of marking cuts is quite important, for two reasons. In auditions or in staging/coaching rehearsals the cuts are easy to read and play through. It also means that, should opening the cut be desired, the single line can be erased easily with little lingering cause for uncertainty. How shortsighted it is of some singers (and pianists) to mark cuts by scribbling out measures in the darkest possible lead or ink, obliterating the entire passage, thus making it absolutely unusable at any time in the future. Audition arias that can be sung with cuts on some days and without cuts on others should be included in two separate editions in an audition folder. That will be covered more extensively later.

The principle of cutting assumes some understanding, too, of why Toscanini and others deemed the complete scores unviable. In operas like *Il Trovatore*, certain cadential or coda sections become excessively long — simply too much of a good thing. Perhaps more properly one should say that much is good and a little is weak or repetitive. In cutting, these passages are shorn of the repetitiveness and are thus strengthened. Purists have been raising their hackles about this lately, but audiences do not object at all to judicious pruning. And yet, an occasionally opened cut is just as delightful, because it is not music that is overly well known. It is a fresh approach to a familiar score.

A difficult gray area to approach is that aspect of coaching which deals with some knowledge of vocal technique. If the coach knows the teaching style and modality of a given teacher and the weaknesses of a given singer, he or she can reinforce the work of the teacher without actually getting into placement, breath support, and so on. Coaches *must have some vocal knowledge.* That way, when the singer is faced with a vocally challenging problem, the coach can give options on how to conquer the problems. Many coaches have accompanied in teachers' studios for the opportunity to learn vocal technique, the teachers sometimes even giving lessons to coaches in exchange for playing lessons. It is a good trade off. The coach might also invest in a book like *The Structure of Singing: System and Art in Vocal Technique* by Richard Miller, which is in the library of voice teachers all over the world.[7] Such a book will give in-depth knowledge to the coach about technique, knowledge he or she can then use in helping singers learn repertoire.

A subject many singers do not understand is "marking." This is simply singing the music lightly, supporting the tone completely but giving little real voice. It may involve taking high notes down an octave or even omitting them. The trick is to mark loudly enough for others to hear necessary cues onstage. Dancers mark, too, by indicating that they are doing cartwheels, and so on, so why shouldn't singers? Some great singers do not like marking, fearing that, when they get tired, they will mark in performance, too. But this is usually not going to be the case. Marking saves singers for the important moments and is a technique they should all learn. Vocal marking does not equate with dramatic marking, which should not be done in staging rehearsals.

I once coached a singer learning the title role in *Lucia di Lammermoor*. She went up for a high D (in "Quando rapito in estasi") and missed it. (As indicated above, everyone expected the high D, so she felt she had to sing it even if Donizetti did not write it.) The note was very tight and collapsed almost immediately. She had attempted a diminuendo as she ascended. I explained to her that it was like pulling the rug out from under her own voice, just when she needed really to go for it with gusto. I agreed that the diminuendo was a wonderful idea but suggested that she should use it as she left the note rather than as she went for it. Success was immediate.

Whether specifically or in principle, a coach must understand the presence of added high notes. Following almost any recording of *Rigoletto* will reveal the addition of many such notes. A coach must understand the reasons they are added and whether they are always added (the line usually seems to aim that way, even if the composer did not write it). A coach must also understand why omitting added higher notes might be an option. Again, digesting the Ricci volumes and careful study of recordings (from various eras of recording if possible) aids in this immeasurably. These added high notes sometimes involve extra breaths, facilitated by dropping some measures vocally. They may also involve understanding that, correct language accent be damned, the high note will be held. In *Turandot*, Calaf's great aria "Nessun dorma" has a fermata on the high B at the end. It is *exciting!* It is ludicrous, however, because "Vincerò" should be accented possibly on the first or, better yet, last syllable, and most certainly not the second one. Yet that is the syllable and note accented, and recorded proof of this distortion extends back to the second generation of singers. Puccini did not write a fermata on the note. A recent attempt to correct this distortion (at the Michigan Opera Theater in 2002) was met with catcalls and booing. Traditionalists are a very stubborn lot!

Occasionally a coach must understand how to help a singer actually have the endurance to get through an entire role. It may involve explaining things like where to give less and where to talk with the conductor about an ideal tempo. Some pieces can be sung at a variety of speeds, while others require certain tempi. This may be because of difficult breaths (tempi that are too fast make phrases shorter, but rests are shortened, too). It is also possible that a certain tempo is required, because some phrases just elude the singer due to their sheer length (a faster tempo might actually help this).

When a singer has a musical problem, the coach must find a way to solve it. In *Un Ballo in Maschera*, Ulrica has some impressive singing to do. But she also has a difficult line in the middle of the big ensemble in her scene, difficult because her line is constantly syncopated. If she breathes in syncopation, she will probably miss the counting and end up on the beat rather than off of it. It might be suggested to her that she breathe rhythmically, *on* the beat, in order to keep the tempo rock solid. If she does this, she will have no problem.

Indeed, solving problems for the singer is probably the most important aspect of coaching. The problems may stem from rhythmic complexities, language, range, or other things. How does a singer, for example, learn to spit out the patter employed by Rossini in *La Cenerentola* at the speed required? It requires a lot of personal practice, repeating over and over at ever-increasing speeds the passage in question. A frequently used term is "muscle memory," and that is quite important when dealing with patter. Muscle memory is simply training the muscles of the mouth to articulate the words at a rapid speed. In Rossini's music the words come so rapidly that the singer's muscles can frequently find the words and articulation before their mind can think of them.

This holds true, as well, in the act 1, scene 2 ensemble of *Falstaff*. It is very difficult to sing in musical terms, and the Italian is quite sophisticated. Added to that is a fast, conversational (arguing) speed that can trip up even the best singers.

Another example of this patter appears in Gilbert and Sullivan patter songs. In their famous patter songs, such as "My name is John Wellington Wells" from *The Sorcerer*, "Modern, Major General" from *The Pirates of Penzance*, and "The Nightmare Song" from *Iolanthe*, one is faced with seeming nonsense that the brain cannot make sensible quickly enough. Lists such as are found in those solos are difficult in and of themselves to memorize, and then having to make sense of them to an audience at such rapid speeds only compounds the problems. The muscular memory helps get the singer through these fast passages with much less stumbling. The only way to achieve such speed, however, is constant, careful practice. Once the speed is attained, then, where possible, the singer can inflect the words with meaning and understanding.

When a singer tries to give too much at either the top or the bottom of his or her range, the author frequently uses the term "optimum roar range," which means that range in which the voice projects easily, with no apparent effort. A voice has certain natural places of focus and projection. At the bottom most voices are weaker, with little or no projection. In the upper middle range of a voice, it is easy for the singer to sing clearly and with a projecting tone at a comfortable volume. A high note usually does not require the amount of volume that many singers expect to penetrate the orchestral fabric. On the other hand, the bottom notes won't come through with immense volume no matter how much effort is expended. They are below that "optimum roar range." This is particularly important to consider when coaching duets. One singer may have to be aware of the other singer's presence in the "nonoptimum roar range." Balancing voices becomes the job of the singers, and helping them understand the need to balance is the responsibility of the coach.

Some other notable vocal and musical problems will be discussed in the chapters directly related to certain composers.

I do not intend to suggest that a coach take voice lessons with the idea that he or she will become a professional singer, but he or she will be dealing with professional, semiprofessional, and even student singers and must know the terminology to use to help the singer negotiate the more difficult passages, whether the difficulty comes from emotional outpouring, rapid passagework, or language.

Any coaching session might involve saying things like "You need to get a better support on that tone" or "You need to shorten that note, so that you can get a good breath for the next phrase." But these are not really technical terms. They are obvious statements, reminders of what the singer should know anyway. A possible technical discussion might involve asking for a slenderer tone to begin a note, one that is more focused and perhaps a little softer in initial volume. This has a way of enabling the singer to crescendo more effectively and to make it to the end of the lengthy note or phrase. Understanding what a slender tone is, however, and what benefit it might have to the singer are the technical knowledge any coach needs, and without that knowledge, the coach will not know to ask for the tonal variety. Other technical areas might include asking for less spread in a tone, a brighter tone, smoother line, and more forward placement of the tone.

A specific example of a technical nature would be found in the ending of the aria "Senza mamma" from *Suor Angelica* by Puccini. The soprano's climactic high A is supposed to be piano fading into nothing. Many singers are used to singing high notes louder than that, but sopranos have a placement, a sort of tonal pocket, in which they can sing a high A which will feel rather small but which will have spin and color without much volume. It carries perfectly and can be sustained for the length requested by Puccini. It is not important that the coach knows how to demonstrate it. What is important is the description of it, and that involves describing the high, almost nasal placement. The note is just above the passaggio of most sopranos, so they can find it easily. (As a tenor myself, I can only *wish* tenors had such a place, but we must resort to head voice or falsetto, which does not match the middle voice as well, so it is not the same effect at all; it cannot be sustained for a long duration either.)

Rapid passagework may involve discussion of support and the origin of good articulation. Many of these things a coach learns for him- or herself by doing it, and before that, from teachers, for whom they accompany or with whom they take lessons. The goal in those voice lessons is not to discover a new Franco Corelli hiding in the vocal folds of an opera coach. The goal is to discover what technique is all about and to learn terminology the coach may use when dealing with a singer outside of the teacher's studio.

This vocal knowledge is all used in helping the singer project the black-and-white and the gray areas of the scores. The coach may not make the decisions about these aspects of the scores, but he or she must know what the traditions are and how a singer must go about creating his or her characters in the best way possible, vocally, musically, and dramatically.

2

RECITATIVES

Practical Methods for Teaching Them

MOST OPERAS HAVE SOME FORM of recitative. The word comes from the Italian term "recitativo" and usually refers to those moments of dialogue in which the musical form and impetus is supplanted by the dramatic needs. It is a piece of sung text, in which the phrasing comes more from the word inflection and meaning than from a musical impulse. "Recitation" thus takes precedence over melody in either aria or arioso (a melodic section lacking formal structure). This does not in any way excuse bad enunciation of thoughts in arias and ensembles. It simply implies that more attention must be paid to the words in recitatives than to musical line. Even the later operas of Verdi, Wagner, and Puccini contain measures or phrases that should be considered recitative in nature.

The recitatives found in operas ranging from the Baroque era up through early Donizetti were predominantly "secco recitatives" — literally "dry recitation." (The Italian word "secco" means the same thing when applied to fine wines — "sec.") The usual definition for this is simple: voice with continuo (harpsichord with cello and/or bass). "Continuo" gives "continuity" to the sung dialogue passages, keeping the singers in a definite tonality and guiding them forward in the changing thoughts that lead to the next musical number. The fact that other chordal instruments such as lute, harpsichord, or even a small organ could play these figured basses, or that other instruments (cello, bass, bassoon, or organ) might play the single written note (mostly written as a whole note) is frequently not mentioned. That is usually an earlier practice. It is generally agreed that the long note should be held a little by the bass instrument, but it should not be held the length indicated. By the early nineteenth century, in the operas of Rossini and Donizetti, the harpsichord or fortepiano supplied the chords without recourse to a sustaining bass instrument at all.

A coach and singer must realize that the chordal realization written in a piano-vocal score (and in most orchestral scores) was, for the most part, not written out by the composer. Composers simply wrote the lowest note of the chord, and expected that the continuo player, frequently the conductor and maybe even the composer himself, would play the chord above it as figured. For a while chords not "figured" were assumed to be "root position" triads (that is to say: 5–3–1). This eventually changed as the chord progressions became more immediately simple and easily understood.

By the time Mozart was writing, in fact, the continuo was written much more freely, with little figuration, and with some freedom as to whether the continuo string(s) should or should not play. Today, particularly in larger auditoriums, a cello is often used to reinforce the volume of the chording instrument. Because of these larger performing venues, microphones are also used to amplify the keyboard instrument, at least for the singers to hear, and, purists not withstanding, pianos and electric harpsichords have been used as well. The point is not exactly what instrument is used, but how the chords are played and their purpose in the first place.

Mozart declared that Italian operas should all have recitatives, that the Italian language sounded unclear if spoken. Most composers seem to have agreed with his opinion. He also felt, however, that German sounded much better spoken and sounded awkward if sung in dialogue passages. Most German operas are either through-composed (not divided into recitative and numbers) and sung throughout, or they have dialogue.

The chord is given to help the singer find and maintain pitches in the recitative. For a coach or harpsichordist, the most satisfactory way of "realizing" the recitative is to roll each given chord quickly, spacing it so that the singer's most prominent pitch is the last one sounded . . . which is to say the top pitch. Usually the rolling is done from the bottom up, but occasionally one can begin at the top, rolling down and back up rapidly. Since the harpsichord dies away quickly, and since long passages sometimes need punctuation, a repeat of the chord (short and not rolled) can sometimes add emphasis to certain words. This takes experimentation. Continual rolling of a chord, unrelated to the words, begins to sound like some kind of concerto, obscuring the words. Instead, the continuo should be helpful and discreet.

The practice of rolling chords on harpsichords possibly began because harpsichord keys do not always respond evenly. Trying to play a chord absolutely together — an easy task in piano playing — may have an inner note sounding slightly earlier or later than other notes in the chord. As this is not a good thing, rolling the chord became a good solution to the problem.

An exit or stage movement can sometimes be "covered" or highlighted with a simple arpeggio or scale. An example of this might be Susanna's exit in act 1 of *Le Nozze di Figaro*, just before Figaro's recitative and aria "Se vuol ballare."

That solo recitative (beginning at "Bravo, signor padrone") is a good example of a place where conductors occasionally add bass instruments to reinforce the prominent bass line. The addition adds gravity to the lines Figaro sings. Even the earlier generations of conductors (those from the 1930s to 1950s), who used harpsichord/piano only for the figured bass, with no cellos or basses, were known to augment the continuo at this point.

The singer's approach to "secco recitativo" should be basically the opposite of what is frequently done. Many singers try to learn the rhythms written by the composer and then try to "free it up," to point up the important words or syllables. Instead, singers should realize that the written rhythms are only the best approximations the composers could devise of natural speech rhythms. These rhythms have also been adjusted (sometimes artificially) by the composers to fit a 4/4 meter. Therefore, if a singer begins by speaking the Italian, giving it meaning and clarity, he or she will probably (after a bit of practice) inflect the words with rhythms quite close to those the composer has given. In rehearsals of Handel operas, in fact, the singers used to practice the recitative passages as dialogue only, pacing them in a quite dramatic and natural way, only getting the notated music a few days before the first performance. (This is another reason the continuo was so important in leading the singers through the correct chordal progressions.)[1]

An older performance practice was that of speeding through the recitatives as fast as a singer could go. This is much like saying a Shakespearean play as fast as you can, with no cognizance given to meaning or to dramatic needs. In recitative the correct speed should be governed by natural speech tempo. This means that if a line needs to be slower to project its meaning, nothing prevents the singer from taking that time. On the other hand, if the singer wants to speed through a passage, he or she can.

Justino Diaz, famous for the roles of Figaro and Don Giovanni, once had to sing in a production of *Le Nozze di Figaro* that was uncut. He made the huge recitative in the second act very funny because he sped through it. In his interpretation, Figaro had his plan, and nothing could possibly derail it — or so he thought. The interpretation worked extremely well. Even those in the audience who spoke not a word of Italian enjoyed the cocksure way in which he did it.

Composers almost never specify a speed for recitative lines! They assume that the singer will understand every word they are singing and inflect them accordingly. There are, however, questions that arise. One of the first questions concerns written rests in the recitative. Often there seems to be no rational reason for their presence or absence. Italians have a predilection for eliding syllables together, and some of the rests are probably there to separate syllables that are better not elided. But other rests are there for no apparent reason. They might be there to make the first syllable after the rest not have an accent, but there is no clear-cut answer. The best rule a coach or singer can follow must be to leave a rest out if it makes absolutely no sense. Great singers of Italian opera (notably, Italians themselves) do this in performance and on recordings, so non-Italians might take a cue from them.

This approach gives the secco recitatives the freedom they require to be correct, a freedom that works every time. After the freedom is there, it is good to review the printed rhythms again to see if the composer has given any important clue to emphasis. It should be obvious that if a composer suddenly shifts from eighths and sixteenths to a string of quarter notes, there must be a reason.

Another rationale for why the above-mentioned recitative before "Se vuol ballare" might include the bass instruments is because the voice part is much more rhythmically specific. It is actually a "recitativo accompagnato," or orchestrally accompanied recitative. In this kind of recitative the orchestra punctuates more completely the sung text, possibly sustaining chords under sung lines and pointing up the changing moods of the text much more completely.

The usual place for a "recitativo accompagnato" is before an aria. Taking *Le Nozze di Figaro* as our basis, "Hai già vinta la causa," "Dove sono," and "Deh vieni, non tardar" are good examples of other arias with a preceding "recitativo accompagnato." The singer has some freedom but must remain quite true to the rhythms given, bending the tempo and rhythms only a little to achieve the word meaning. Since this has a more Romantic feel to it, singers have less trouble with this style of recitative. Unfortunately, they sometimes become less specific in the "pointing" of words, and this is the opposite of what the practice should entail. The orchestra is used to underline the sung text, commenting in ways on the depth and colors of the character's thoughts. Therefore what is sung cannot be generic in nature. The dynamic taken for any given line may answer an orchestral punctuation at the same general volume, or it may anticipate the next orchestral phrase with a change of volume or articulation that the orchestra will use in answer.

When one thinks of either type of recitative, one should be reminded of a phrase spoken by Don Andrès in Offenbach's operetta *La Périchole*. At one point in act 1, he enters, saying (here in English translation), "O truth, truth, where are you truth?" In recitative it is the singer's duty to give truth and meaning to every word.

It is important to note, too, that, though it does not apply to the secco recitative, a curious axiom holds true particularly in the accompanied recitatives of opera: The composer wrote the rests, too. Verdi and Donizetti used rests as marvelous moments for collecting thoughts, for surveying situations before commenting on them. Many a young singer rushes through these, wishing to get to the "important" part (the words), without realizing how absolutely pregnant such pauses and moments for reflection can be.

In later operas, those which are from the Romantic period, recitatives may become more arioso (melodic and rhythmically specific). But the drama comes through in these moments, too. Word projection must not be slighted. Communication is the most important part of being a singer.

To work with all these styles, a coach should have the singer speak the lines with as much meaning as possible. One potential exercise, which aids immensely in text projection and understanding, is to say a line switching from one language to the other and back. An example (again from *Figaro*) might be:

"Where are they, those beautiful moments?"

or:

"Dove are they, those bei momenti?"

or:

"Where sei, i beautiful moments?"

Stress to singers that linguistic cognates are their friends. In the above example, "momenti" and "moments" are cognates — words that are close enough in one language for a singer, thinking in another language, to have a real emotional response, even if they do not really know the language per se. A few basic examples of foreign words and their corresponding cognates will help to explain.

French	Italian	German	English
fleur	*fiore*	*Blume*	*flower or bloom*
démon	*demonio*	*Teufel*	*demon or devil*
lasse	*lascia*	*lassen*	*let or allow*
lettre	*lettera*	*Brief*	*letter or legal brief*
commande	*commadare*	*Kommandieren*	*command*
deux	*due*	*zwei*	*two*
mon	*mio*	*mein*	*my or mine*

In the above list, it is easy to see that not all languages will give up the same cognate, but just as obviously some are quite close from one language to another.

The required volume for recitative is not great — in fact, most singers tend to oversing secco recitative. Even Mozart complained that singers "sang" too much, so the problem is not new. However, the solution is not talking on pitches, because a voice must be supported and produced properly in order to project to the back wall. When a voice is accompanied only by the continuo, great volume is simply not required. The easiest solution to the problem is the elimination of legato "line," the lyric binding together of notes in a smooth and uninterrupted phrase. This is what all singers work years to achieve, and such line is appropriate in the "cantilenas" (literally "singing lines") of Bellini or Mozart. But particularly secco recitative requires no line. Recitativo accompagnato requires only a little more line, moments here and there rising to emotionally sustained levels. Approaching the recitatives with less line but continued support and placement, the voice retains its colors and its projective capabilities without becoming a sustained garble of held pitches and indefinite diction. A badly produced voice, which has no natural line left, will still sound bad in recitative, because the voice is not "speaking" clearly on any given pitch.

Donizetti used yet a different method to deal with dialogue. He would compose an orchestral theme played behind the parlando singing of the characters. (Parlando means "speaking quality.") The opening of *Don Pasquale* shows this well, as does the music both before and after the sextet in *Lucia di Lammermoor*. In those places the singer must sing with a full tone and with only a semblance of line. The singer, though not usually singing something one would call a melody, may actually take notes here and there that are part of the melody the orchestra is playing. It is something between accompanied recitative and arioso (which has some real melodic interest) and can seamlessly lead into the next musical "number."

In the verismo operas, dramatic utterance is of paramount importance. Since "verismo" means "realism," this means that formal, musical concerns frequently are of less importance than the sweeping emotions. The "truth" of the dramatic situations blurs the distinctions made by earlier composers between recitative and the musical "number." (In a "numbers opera," arias and ensembles have a definite beginning and a clearly delineated sense of close.) Most of the operas of Puccini, Leoncavallo, Mascagni, or Giordano include passages of a kind of recitative. The opening of act 4 of *Andrea Chenier*, for example, or of act 4 of *La Bohème* are actually recitative passages. They are perhaps more strictly sung in tempo, but they still retain the sense of real dialogue. The musical numbers that follow have a clear beginning and ending and are divorced from the surrounding "dialogue."

A strange mixture can be found in Smetana's *The Bartered Bride* where there are recitatives that were originally dialogue. In revising the dialogue for inclusion as sung recitative, Smetana wrote in an almost secco style, albeit accompanied with orchestra. Donizetti's *Don Pasquale* takes a similar course, though it never had dialogue. This kind of parlando passage allows a little tempo freedom, but almost no rhythmic freedom. If singers are allowed to take too much rhythmic freedom, they will find that, rather than clarifying the words and intentions, they will make things more muddled. The singer needs to learn the passages rhythmically as they are learning the words and notes.

One question in recitatives that arises in music from Donizetti back through at least Handel and Vivaldi is what to do with appoggiaturas. If the composers expected appoggiaturas, why didn't they write them? The answer to that is that the dissonance on the beat was anathema to the theory of the time. So, rather than officially break rules, they wrote with appoggiaturas in mind, expecting them to be inserted unofficially. There are certain rules concerning them and their application. The first rule concerns the written leap downward or upward of a third on a strong beat. When descending, the third should be filled in. (See Figure 5a.) If ascending, the third may be filled in, or the upper neighbor of the written pitch may be substituted. (See Figure 5b.) This may even be done in ascending seconds, in which the chromatic note between the written pitches may be substituted. (See Figure 5c.)

The other major appoggiatura to be dealt with is that of the descending fourth or fifth. The leap downward of a fourth or fifth onto the strong beat is frequently jarring, seeming like terrible voice leading. Instead the upper note of the interval is repeated and the descent is delayed by one note. This gives the strong beat emphasis, which the written pitches seem to avoid. (See Figure 5d.) The other method of dealing with this problem is to change several more pitches. This may seem like heresy, but many recitatives were written in great haste (and sometimes not by the composer), and the larger change simply seems more natural. (See Figure 5e.)

Appoggiaturas are not usually performed if the drop is on a monosyllabic word. Italian of course has some words (like "mio"), which can be considered mono- or bisyllabic in nature. When monosyllabic words are given appoggiaturas, the resulting whine as the notes move seems wrong. A notable exception can be found at the end of "Comfort ye" from Handel's *Messiah*, where the word "God" is usually given two pitches.

This covers most of the problems associated with recitatives. The next few chapters will cover planning coaching sessions, following a conductor, coaching from the perspective of the stage manager, and singers auditioning and how coaches can help them in that trying exercise. In Part 2, I will deal with specific problems associated with the Baroque, Mozart, Rossini and the bel canto movement, French opera, Verdi, Richard Wagner and Richard Strauss, Mussorgsky and other Russians, operettas, and twentieth-century composers such as Britten. The Interludes will deal with smaller but still important issues. Some of what will be said may fly in the face of thought on styles of singing, but it is all based on practical work with singers in this repertoire.

Figures 5a-e Handel — *Alcina M* excerpts.

INTERLUDE ONE

DECORUM

Webster's Dictionary defines "decorum" as: 1. whatever is suitable or proper; propriety; congruity; 2. propriety and good taste in behavior, speech, dress, etc.; 3. *often in pl.* an act or requirement of polite behavior.[1]

In conducting and coaching, that means taking a somewhat stiff stance toward the people with whom you work. For example, a conductor should either memorize the names of every member of the orchestra, or he should refer to them by the position they play (i.e., 1st trombone, 1st stand viola, piccolo, etc.). The concertmaster may be addressed by first name, but it becomes awkward if the conductor refers to the 3rd horn by name and addresses the 1st horn by his position. The conductor or coach must keep all activities on a professional basis. The unforgivable slip in decorum that is most frequently committed is the personal attack, frequently combined with sarcasm.

As John Donne put it so eloquently, "No man is an island." For that reason it is important to realize that music is a reflection of life. Both are ensemble efforts and cannot be accomplished well without the input of other musicians. With the isolated exceptions of electronic music, solo piano literature, and unaccompanied works for solo instruments, all other music making is a collaborative effort. The compositions of electronic music raise the distaste of some people in part because it is a fixed art form with no possibility of spontaneity.

With this collaboration in mind, it is important for any musician to realize that, unless a person is not even trying to be a good musician, patience should be the overriding factor in all rehearsals. It may, of course, be necessary to apply professional pressure in order to get things accomplished. Some pieces and people need extra effort to reach acceptable performance levels. But assuming a musician is working at his or her capacity, it is not a good thing to become impatient with a colleague. Such impatience leads to tensions and impedes progress toward the ideal goal.

When working as a coach or conductor, it is important to keep things on a positive note. The effort to put music together may occasionally make things tense, but it serves no one to allow those tensions to degenerate into snide sarcasm and petty comments. Saying things like "I'm just not used to working on this level" or "I was expecting to work with musicians, not children" (I have heard both!) serves only the ego of the one making the comment and generates terrible feelings and higher tensions as a result.

At some point it may be necessary to discuss privately, either with an individual in question or with collaborative colleagues, problems being faced. But such sessions are about finding solutions to impediments to the desired perfection in the music making. They are *not* about personality slander. The coach who is unwilling to work with a singer because he or she is "stupid" will find that the real problem lies more in the coach than with the singer. Some of the greatest singers in opera have a difficult time learning music.

Finding a way through a singer's protective armor may take greater effort than expected, but any musician will bristle if attacked personally rather than on a professional level. In music rehearsals coaches and conductors must always remember to work with the problem and not simply to denigrate the person creating the problem. I have learned that finding a way to make things correct can open the door for a singer to be a far greater artist than early coaching sessions might indicate. I have also learned that resorting to sarcasm creates only hard feelings.

There may come a time when it becomes obvious that a singer just does not have the musical knowledge and background to learn a specific role in the allotted time. Then it will take great tact to rectify the problem by replacing the singer, because such efforts can lead to hard feelings and personal confrontations. Other cast members may have built friendships with the replaced singer and feel threatened by the replacement. The more professionally the musical staff reacts, the more comfortable the transition to a different singer will be for all concerned.

3

PLANNING COACHING SESSIONS, PLAYING STAGING REHEARSALS, AND FOLLOWING A CONDUCTOR

SALIERI'S OPERA *PRIMA LA MUSICA, POI LE PAROLE* covers one basic question well. Which should come first, words or music? In coaching, it depends! One singer will assimilate a role in a different way from the next singer. Some prefer working on notes, slighting words and rhythms at first then picking those up completely in later sessions. Other singers cannot function well without the words being accurate. The experienced singer will know what he or she needs and can help plan a coaching session. But with younger singers (and even with some professional ones) the coach is frequently the best judge of how to approach any given piece of music, including knowledge of those numbers that are certain to cause major problems in learning.

If the music is relatively straightforward, the coach might choose to go directly through one portion; an entire duet, an aria, or even a larger ensemble can be covered, with the idea of getting the singer used to the shape of the whole. Then the coach and singer work on specific errors, things in need of work. These may include correcting rhythms, mispronunciations, pitches, subtle nuances, and dynamics.

Rhythms may need firming up. If performance tradition conflicts with the printed page, discussion should develop over which should take precedence. The composer's printed text is always the starting point, but Baroque music in particular includes passages in which the printed text is not followed. Such passages usually involve the singer's rhythms being different from those printed in the orchestral accompaniment: a melodic passage might be even in the voice and dotted in the orchestra. Whether the voice should also dot becomes the point of discussion. (See Figure 6a.) Even modern popular music has such things in the unequal eighth notes of jazz rhythms. (See Figure 6b.)

Figure 6(a) Handel — *Alcina* — "Chi m'insegna" — shown as written and as it might possibly be sung.

Figure 6(b) "*Honeysuckle Rose*," words by Andy Razaf, music by Tomas Waller — © 1929 Chappell.

But rhythms that need to be followed must be corrected. Singers may not see a reason for even rhythms versus dotted rhythms. But the answer can always be that the composer *did* see a reason. The argument may pale a bit when dealing with translations, but the impulse of the rhythm frequently makes a big difference in the force of a piece of music. In Verdi's *Il Trovatore*, if Leonora does not scrupulously dot the rhythms in the "Miserere," the effect can be quite sluggish and boring.

Some coaches even encourage not following the printed score. In "Vedrai, carino," from *Don Giovanni*, Mozart has Zerlina sing "qua" several times. In the penultimate phrase, she ends with two "quas" in a row. Some coaches feel that this sounds too much like a duck, eliminating the last "qua." But, since it *can* be sung beautifully, and since Mozart clearly knew what he was doing, my personal feeling is that it should be sung as written.

Singers have an uncanny ability to mangle languages when they don't know the language itself very well. It is perhaps understandable for a singer to insert inadvertently an additional *n* in the Italian word "costanza," making it into "constanza." This added letter is called a "false friend." The inserted letter is usually one appearing elsewhere in the word, and the singer simply repeats it, possibly being unsure of the exact spelling and pronunciation of the word. An added *r* or *l* can creep into any number of words. Part of the problem comes from the old habit of learning words by rote, with no sense of verbal meaning or continuity. Even great singers have confessed to rote learning. However, if a singer of the role of Adina sings "d'isparmi" instead of "d'ispirarmi" in the first duet with Nemorino, it is simply careless study and must be corrected. Some corrections are necessary, too, where doubled consonants make a difference. In *Le Nozze di Figaro*, if Cherubino (in "Non so più") sings "ogni dona" instead of "ogni donna," the difference is important. One means "every gift" and the other means "every woman." While Cherubino may indeed think of every woman as a gift, it is still not what he is singing. Professional singers can make just as many errors as students.

In Despina's "Una donna" aria (*Così fan Tutte*), she must be careful to sing the word "anni" and not "ani." The former is "years" and the second is "ass/donkey!"

The German composer Richard Wagner is said to have counseled singers to pay attention to the small notes, that the large notes take care of themselves. His point is aptly taken. The main notes of a melody as sung are seldom wrong, but pickup notes and passagework frequently derail due to singers learning haphazardly. Some of this faulty learning comes from studying roles by listening for hours to recordings, which are not infallible. Singers of great repute make mistakes right and left on our favorite CDs, and studying them will reinforce their errors in a new generation of singers. The hearing of singers also frequently allows them to substitute what they think the recorded performer is singing and not the true notes the recording represents. Using recordings for learning notes is not a good idea. Using them for study of styles, older traditions, and the like can be a wonderful idea. As Tibor Kozma said, "Study recordings before or after — but not instead of."[1] By that he meant to study recordings before personal study of a role (learning the shape and general tempi), then listen for new ideas after the role is learned, but one should never use the recording to learn the notes and interpretation of a role.

It should be pointed out that mistakes, once learned, are much harder to throw out and relearn correctly. This is particularly true in the difficult works of Rossini or Handel. Passagework, such as is found in every character in *La Cenerentola*, must be clean and accurate. This is the reason new critical editions are emerging. Singers cannot learn the correct pitches if they are not in print.

Dynamics are vitally important. For a few years, the great singers seemed to sing in dynamics ranging from forte to fortissimo. The softest dynamic sung was no less than mezzo forte. Now, with the return of ensemble operas to the repertory and stronger-willed conductors (and more conscientious singers!), dynamics are being reinforced. Even the standard repertoire works, which used to be bellowed to the rafters, are now tailored to the printed dynamics. This saves singers in ways they can hardly imagine, and it also gives wonderful shape to every number. The mitigating problem with good dynamics is the huge halls which economics demand for operas today. Still, even the Metropolitan Opera (seating capacity of around 4,000) is reviewing dynamics with good results, and ensembles gain an incredible clarity and balance if the singers are not all trying for the loudest volume that they can produce.[2]

Coaches also must frequently insist on proper note length. Unaccented syllables are sometimes held meaninglessly far beyond their printed values, proving that the singer either does not know the language well or does not care. The error is almost never the result of compositional excess but stems from the singer landing on the syllable and simply not thinking about the natural inflection of the words. Even the accented syllables are sometimes held double or triple the values printed. This does not refer to the vocal display of holding the last note of an aria.

Cast musical sense aside there, since it's a "moment" for the singer. But holding the last note of an internal phrase may clash with harmonies, be unstylistic, and may rob singers of needed moments of rest. Besides, the composer did not write it that way!

There is also the fact that coaching sessions must address ensembles, both in helping the solo singers find their notes and rhythms, but also in putting such ensembles together. The solo coaching sessions must never concentrate only on the solo numbers, however important these may be. Inner voices in ensembles must be rehearsed carefully. An ensemble must be sung with good diction, all consonants exploding together, all vowels matching, and with all passages exactly together. Inaccurate notes or rhythms must be corrected to ensure the true meaning of the word "ensemble."

Articulations in ensembles also must be enforced and balanced. Many composers wrote with different articulations for the various characters in an ensemble. This helps to delineate one character or group of characters from another. An ensemble such as the "Awakening" section of the act 1 finale of *Così fan Tutte* is just such an ensemble.

When two or more texts are sung simultaneously, it will help immensely if singers point phrases to the important words. The coach will sometimes have to help the singers find words that are not accented at exactly the same place as the next character. Then the shifting focus of important words from one singer to another makes much more of the text understandable. Ensembles like those found in act 1, scene 2 of Verdi's *Falstaff* can actually be made clear in this fashion. It may not be possible to follow all five texts at once, but something like three texts will emerge clearly enough to follow.

The coach in an opera company is frequently called upon to arrange ensemble rehearsals. These will include duets, trios, quartets, and, sometimes, fuller ensembles (minus chorus). A scene like the auto-da-fé in *Don Carlos* by Verdi is a mass of shifting rhythms, tempi, and emotions. Even without a music director/conductor present, the coach may have to hold sessions to put the disparate elements together, explaining the piece occasionally measure by measure so that everyone understands the shape.

None of those love duets (over which audiences swoon) fall together by themselves. It is not only a simple matter of making notes fit together. Questions arise of tempo, mood, shape and balance, and both volume and structure. The Duke and Gilda in *Rigoletto*; Carlo, Eboli, and Posa in *Don Carlo*; the three ladies in *Die Zauberflöte*; the rustics in *A Midsummer Night's Dream* by Britten; and the quintet from *Carmen* are but a few examples of ensembles needing considerable practice.

The latter issue also brings up a rehearsal device. The speed required for the *Carmen* quintet is incredible, yet noted singers have said that, once the number is learned, the diction and speed are not so terribly difficult to achieve. One cannot start rehearsing at full speed! Each member of the quintet must start slowly to get the words into his or her mouth. It may be necessary to begin using only words, no notes. Then, as speed is gradually gained, the notes can be added, too. The quick interchange between voices is yet another part of the problem in that famed number. In initial rehearsals, the coach needs to have everyone practice it rather mechanically. The meaning and inflections of words can be dealt with later. Starting too soon on the "drama" of the piece will probably mean the singers will never be technically secure. The Figaro who starts acting his way through "Largo al factotum" before gaining the vocal control of the piece will run into major problems. Once the physical efforts are mastered, the subtleties of the words are addressed, including attitudes like sarcasm, flattery, amorous intentions, or anger.

A number like the delightful argument in act 2 of Sondheim's *Into the Woods*, "Your Fault," is best rehearsed as rhythm divorced from pitches. Every time a singer says the words, "So it's your fault," he or she must point to the person being blamed. When the notes are added (and then the staging), this type of preparation will serve to make the number quite secure.

There will of course come the day when the conductor enters the picture. The coach, in anticipation of that day, should rehearse quicker and slower tempos, keeping the singers flexible. Setting a tempo or delivery of a line too soon may actually inhibit musical or dramatic exploration of the score. The conductor will probably have slightly different ideas and so will the stage director. Conductors are the guiding light for any production. If that light is sometimes dim, it is not for the coach to say. The conductor enters and begins shaping the whole opera as he or she sees fit. He or she has presumably studied musical styles and the thrust of the drama, and must help make the stage director's vision come to life. At this point a good coach is absorbing as much as possible the exact tempi the conductor sets, getting those tempi into his or her body for those later rehearsals when the conductor may not be available. The coach may even write into the score, "a little faster" or "more sustained." This only means that, for that coach, the conductor is taking a slightly faster or more sustained tempo than the coach expected.

The coach also shifts a little at this moment from coach to "orchestral player," because it is no longer the coach's job to help shape the singers. The conductor is there for that as is the director. The coach now must follow every tempo change as expertly as possible. Listening to the singing is no longer his or her job (at least in theory). The coach is now supposed to reflect to the best of his or her ability the sound that will issue from the pit.

Following the tempo set by a conductor is not really such a difficult task. The coach keeps that tempo, watching the conductor peripherally until the conductor changes that tempo. Dynamics may come from the conductor but are also printed on the page. Careful reproduction of those dynamics will help reinforce in the singers what they will hear (and what dynamics they should be singing). At this stage, it may become clear that certain singers are having problems not due directly to the presence of the conductor. If a singer has pitch concerns, the coach needs to point those out. It is not that the conductor is incapable of hearing such things, but the conductor's job may be on a different musical plane at that moment. The coach can take a singer aside and point out pitch problems without undue attention being drawn to the singer. If singers have difficulties in dealing with certain entrances or rhythms, it may be incumbent on the coach to find a solution. One very good solution to some of these is the rhythmic subtext.

In drama a subtext might be defined as a text being thought while other words are being spoken. In opera, there are frequently melodic (and rhythmic) passages leading into a vocal entrance. These reflect the ideas the singer should be thinking at that moment. If the singer will give those melodies a text that leads up to their entrance, they should have no problem making the tricky entrance accurately. This text is thought rhythmically but not sung. A good example comes from *Don Giovanni*. In the aria "Vedrai, carino," Zerlina is asked to wait two measures between her phrase, "sentilo battere, sentilo battere," and "toccami qua." Many singers try to sing one measure earlier than they should. The very next phrase is exactly like the one just sung, except that the two empty measures are now sung with the text "sentilo — battere." If Zerlina simply *thinks* that text during the first phrase, she won't make the mistake again.

During piano rehearsals conductors must sometimes stop conducting in order to make notes, but this does not mean that the coach should stop playing. The coach must follow the conductor explicitly when he is conducting, however. The conductor in rehearsals may make mistakes, and the conductor may not follow the singer as the singer might like. The coach is to follow the conductor and not the singer. The conductor may not be following the singer on purpose, trying to get the singer to follow him! If the conductor makes an error due to a distraction, rather than let a rehearsal come to a screeching halt, the coach is advised to help a little, although this kind of help must be momentary.

A coach may have differing ideas on how to improve any given number, but it is not the coach's job at that moment to put forth his or her ideas. At some break in a staging or musical rehearsal, he or she might raise a question, give a suggestion. But the conductor may have very good reasons not to do certain things. Even if the conductor's refusal to take a suggestion is based on their lack of knowledge of the score or their own insecure paranoia, it does not matter. The conductor rules the music. If a tempo is too slow or too fast, it is the director's job to make suggestions and is not the job of the coach.

One conductor, who shall go nameless, was once conducting a production of *La Traviata*. During the Violetta/Germont duet in act 2, at the words "Ah il supplizio è si spietato ...," the conductor took the *Ancora più vivo* with emphasis on the *vivo*. It had a severe, headlong rush. The director and singers all complained that the tempo was too fast. When the coach mentioned the same thing, the conductor asked, rather belligerently, *why* it was too fast. The coach pointed out that, at that tempo, the dissonances, which Verdi places later in the passage, go by so quickly that they don't register. Rather than creating more tension, the quicker tempo lessened the tension. The conductor agreed with this evaluation, and he slowed the tempo to the traditional one.

Coaches take note: It is not always just the suggestion that is made, but it may be in part the tone used in giving the suggestion!

4

THE STAGE DIRECTOR'S PERSPECTIVE

(*THIS CHAPTER WAS WRITTEN BY* **Victoria Vaughan** *for this volume and covers the work of the coach and of others from a different perspective.*)

The coach accompanist is a vital member of any opera staging rehearsal and is often the primary link between the musical staff and the production team. Staging usually begins once the coach has already worked with the singers and has briefed them on the tempi, rubato, and nuances of the conductor's interpretation, in addition to stylistic considerations and other musical preparation. Generally, the coach accompanist plays the piano (or harpsichord) for stagings, with the conductor or chorus master/mistress present to establish the contact between the "orchestra" (piano) and the stage. Sometimes a coach will be required to play the piano without a conductor present, and occasionally several members of coaching staff will be involved, so that, for example, one coach might conduct while another plays the piano.

The following sections cover the process of opera stagings and suggest how the coach accompanist can best prepare for these rehearsals.

1. PRODUCTION PERSONNEL

The **stage director**[1] works with a design team to create the production *concept* for the piece and is involved with talking to the singers about their individual characters in light of this concept. He or she uses the staging sessions to give singers their *blocking*: where to be on the stage at any moment in the opera and how to motivate their movements onstage dramatically. Additionally, the director will help the singers to relate to each other's characters.

The **director's** main responsibility is to tell the story to the audience, and this is the primary goal of the staging rehearsals. Because each scene has a different level of dramatic intensity (though this does not necessarily coincide with the musical score), the director is the person who plans how each rehearsal period will be used. Stagings vary in length but are typically three hours long. It is worth remembering that recitative takes longer to stage than arias or ensemble pieces, because recitatives present considerably more dramatic material to the audience. More staves on each page may give the impression that more pages will be covered in each staging, but this also does not follow, especially where a large, bustling chorus is involved. As a rule, ten pages of recitative and aria will take up one three-hour staging session. This time period could include:

A musical run-through at the start of the rehearsal, to remind the singer about the conductor's interpretation of the section to be staged.

Basic "blocking out" of the scene. Initially, this will probably be done without music; then sections of the music will be added and may be repeated.

Reviewing the blocking and running through the scene with the music.

Final alterations of the stage "picture" by the director.

The director relies on the coach accompanist to provide an accurate indication of the tempi and dynamics, so that they can use this to determine the dramatic pace of the opera. Generally, a staging covers consecutive pages of the score, and the coach will usually begin at the top of the section and play it in segments until the assigned pages have been blocked. This often involves playing the same section of the opera over again and again; such repetition should be expected, as it is a vital part of the process for the singers, who are learning the director's interpretation for the very first time.

Although the director is the person who decides on the content of each staging, the **stage manager** (SM) and **assistant stage manager(s)** (ASM[s]) are in charge of the actual execution of this time. Rehearsals in opera houses where contracts are created in accordance with union regulations are the strictest about the use of rehearsal time, and the SM is responsible for facilitating this. Much of the SM's work is done ahead of the stagings. Initially, he or she will be given the scenic details in the form of floor plans, to be used to "tape out" the floor of the rehearsal studio. This can be a complex task, because scenery often has several different levels. There may be steps up to different "floors" of a building, or sections of the set that move on wheels (wagons).

The SM may share with the director the responsibility of presenting visual materials to the singers, such as pictures of the scenery and sketches of the costumes, and explaining the colored tape on the floor that denotes acting areas. SMs also help the singers with the practical elements of staging, by providing them with the necessary props and costume pieces. Many companies will use "rehearsal props and costumes" — that is, props that represent the item but are just for rehearsals. Examples of these include scrolls of paper, where using the real item would damage it long before the final performance. The most common rehearsal costume items are rehearsal skirts, which allow the singer to get the feel of wearing a long skirt while traversing the stage. Singers particularly like to work with rehearsal corsets if they will be wearing them in performance, because it is important for them to become accustomed to the restraints on the ribcage. Male singers will often wear rehearsal jackets, such as tailcoats and vests, for a similar reason. Sneakers are not useful rehearsal shoes because the wearer tends to move very differently in them (normally with added bounce). Women may wear "character shoes" and men often wear an old pair of formal shoes. This affects the stance and vocal production in addition to movement, which is why singers like to wear them from the first day of staging onward.

The stage management team works in close contact with the coaching staff, especially in the final stages of rehearsal. The most common interaction is with regard to starting places in the score during rehearsals, so that the SM staff can follow the stage action closely and make note of entrances and prop use. This is especially important once the rehearsals have moved to the theater, when the piano is in the orchestra pit and in close contact with the maestro, while the stage manager is on the side of the stage and effectively out of contact with the musical staff.

The **assistant director(s)** spends much of the early rehearsals taking down notes about the blocking, so that he or she has a visual record in the score about where each person is onstage, which props they are holding, and other important information about the staging. Later in the process it is not unusual for the AD to work individually with certain singers on elements of dramatic detail. This may happen in a different location from the main staging, and a coach may be assigned to work with the AD for these times. The AD of a new production is invariably the person who restages the show to go on tour or at a new venue if the original director cannot stage it. If there is no AD, the SM staff will absorb these responsibilities.

A **choreographer** will probably be involved with any opera that has even a small amount of dancing. The choreographer might have his or her own troupe of dancers, or perhaps a single dancer to perform a small instrumental section of the piece. Sometimes the choreographer is employed to work with the chorus members, either to teach them a dance (such as a waltz for *Die Fledermaus*, or a mazurka in *Yevghenyi Onegin*), or to instruct them in posture and stylistic necessities. Some companies will employ a pianist who works only with the dancers, but many will use a coach accompanist for short choreographed sections. One important thing to note here is that dancers are not usually versed in the same musical vocabulary as singers and pianists. For one thing, counting "beats" tend to occur in divisions of eight (rather than four) and often choreographers will group two or more measures together for the purpose of creating their dances. In other words, dancers will feel a sixteen-bar phrase as a unit of eight beats. If you are in doubt, play the music on the piano or sing it to the choreographer, to clarify where it is that they want you to start or stop playing. In doing so, you will also help any singers who are involved in the dance to know how the musical parameters tie in with the footwork. As always, be sure to keep detailed notes about tempi: If you play at a tempo that is too fast for dancers, they might injure themselves. An excessively slow tempo is equally dangerous, especially if there are lifts involved in the routine.

2. THE REHEARSAL PROCESS

Each rehearsal is planned to make best use of the time and resources available. Scheduling for the rehearsal will therefore be based on room size and availability, which scenes need blocking according to which singers are available and when, the needs of the maestro and chorus master, and technical considerations such as whether it is practical to move from one scenic setup to the next in order (or to take scenes in a different order to speed up the set change). When you arrive early for the rehearsal, make sure that the piano is in a sensible place for you to be able to see both the action and the conductor.

At the start of each staging, the maestro or the maestro's assistant may request a musical run-through of the pages that are being covered for that rehearsal. This is most likely for a first staging of a given scene, but does not normally happen for review sessions or a full run of an act. If the singers are not already familiar with the stage, the scenery will be explained, often with photographs of previous productions if it is "in repertory" scenery. Drawings of the floor plan will show an aerial view of the stage, while renderings will illustrate a frontal-view picture (sometimes in color with characters drawn in) to show how it looks from the audience's perspective. This might all seem unimportant for the coach accompanist, but there are several reasons to pay attention to these details. Singers up on high platforms onstage will react very differently to the conductor than if they are downstage in front of his nose, and it is part of the coach's job to be aware of this. It will help you when you need to assist their musical preparation of difficult staging elements.

3. VOCABULARY

There are a few words and phrases that you need to know before we get to your first imaginary staging. Production staff uses many of these words as if they are part of normal English parlance, which can be frustrating to the novice coach accompanist. After a few weeks, you will find yourself using them fluently, but the list below will give you a head start:

"Cross Stage Left" or "Stage Right":
This refers to the direction in which an actor walks, as seen from his or her perspective while facing the conductor. When the audience sees the singer "crossing stage left," it means that the singer is going to the audience's right-hand side. If you need to refer to the stage manager's score for singer's blocking, you will often see XSL or XSR written as shorthand.

"He crosses upstage and she counters downstage":
A bit of history here, from when stages were higher at the back than they were at the front (before the audience seats were built in tiers). In this example, if the male actor "crosses upstage" and away from the audience, the female will "counter" (go the other way) by walking toward the audience. A sloping stage is called a "raked stage" and is made wedge-shaped by constructing a large platform that sits on top of the actual stage.

Legs, Wings, and Cycs:
The legs are the long curtains of black fabric that hang on either side of the stage. The gap between each leg is called a wing and is numbered by

the SM, with the lowest number being the furthest downstage (called L.1 or R.1 for short). A cyclorama (or cyc) hangs along the back of the stage and curves downstage at the sides. Rather than being painted (as a backdrop in the same position would be) the screen has lights projected onto it, and the lights or image comes from behind. If it is flat rather than curved, it is called a rear projector (RP) screen. A scrim is a huge piece of fabric that often covers the entire proscenium opening at the front of the stage. Up close it can be seen that the fabric is one piece of seamless netting that has one particularly useful property: if the lighting is turned on behind the scrim, the fabric "disappears," but if it is lit from the front you cannot see the stage behind it. This allows the scenery or actors to move behind the scrim undetected by the audience. Despite the physical barrier, the singers will hear the coach or orchestra perfectly well from behind a scrim, and they will have no problem seeing the conductor. Other common scenic elements include raised platforms, step units, and flats (walls made by stretching a canvas over a large wooden frame).

There are several excellent books that cover technical stage terms in detail. Ionazzi 1992[2] has a good dictionary of terms for all theatrical use, while Clark 2002[3] is designed specifically for advanced opera students.

4. ANATOMY OF A STAGING

Synopsis:

Carmen has been warned by her gypsy friends that Don José, her old lover, is in the area and has been behaving strangely. Defiantly, she chooses to meet him outside the bullring where her new lover, Escamillo (the Toreador), is winning a bullfight. Don José has a fiery temper and cannot believe that Carmen has betrayed him. He tries to remind her of the love they once shared and convince her not to leave him, but Carmen declares that she will live and die a free woman. The offstage chorus then sings of Escamillo's impending victory, and Don José realizes that Carmen is truly in love with Escamillo. He confronts her with this accusation until she admits that it is true.

The following excerpt is an illustration of how a director might approach part of the final scene of Bizet's *Carmen*. Most scenes are considerably longer than this example, but it shows you the level of detail that needs to be covered for a potentially frenetic segment of action. This particular excerpt involves only two characters onstage, and there are not usually any large scenic units onstage due to the required size of the chorus/parade at the start of this scene. Let us imagine that there is a door at the rear of the stage leading to an imaginary bullring, but that otherwise the stage is bare.

During a staging, the director will normally indicate where each dramatic moment starts by referring to the text or the musical material. He or she may ask for the accompanist to play a segment of the music on the piano, especially if it is to be finely choreographed, or if there is any stage combat where the precise timing of the action is vital for safety. The phrases are staged individually or in clusters then strung together, and finally the entire segment is rehearsed fully a few times. Considering that this is a one-minute musical example from a three-hour opera, you get some idea of the level of repetition that can be required. A staging of this scene would take approximately 10–15 minutes to complete, including questions from the actors and musical comments from the coach or maestro.

Take a few minutes to look at the example below (Figure 7), and perhaps play the piano-vocal score before and after reading the stage directions, to see how it all fits together. You might also listen to some recordings to see how the offstage choral elements are closely tied in with this particular staging. Nineteen sections are labeled on the score; these correlate with the numbered items below and illustrate how a director might break the scene into dramatic phrases. Each staging direction is followed by comments in italics that suggest how the action may affect the musical presentation.

> **Measure 3.** Don José stands between Carmen and her exit (through the door to the bullring). She looks for a way to get around him but cannot find one. *Luckily, our bullring door is upstage; this is helpful when the tenor is hoping to catch a musical cue for his first note, as Carmen will automatically be downstage of him.*
>
> **Measure 7.** Don José looks into Carmen's eyes, but she turns away to avoid eye contact, which might give away her secret love for Escamillo. *Free tempo here allows the actors to create tension as she looks away from his gaze.*
>
> **Measure 9.** She walks around him to try and exit, but he grabs her arm. *Again, recitative timing allows them to maneuver the grasp safely.*
>
> **Measure 10.** He grabs her other hand, so that she stands directly in front of him for the fermata *(allowing for connection with the pit).*
>
> **Measure 11.** She pulls away from his grasp. *This might occur at any time in the music, but if it happens on the word "jamais" it will add strength to the text.*

Figure 7   Bizet — Excerpt from *Carmen* (Act IV).

Measure 14. She begins to walk around him; she feels very self-assured about the ease with which she is leaving him. *She will walk upstage of him so that she can face downstage and sing out.*

Measure 16. They both stop moving at the sound of the fanfare and the noise of the chorus who claim Escamillo's victory. They both look in the direction of the sound. *Eye contact between soloists and conductor is not required during the offstage chorus. This*

2

Figure 7 (continued). Bizet — Excerpt from *Carmen* (Act IV).

> facilitates their turn upstage and allows them complete freedom of
> movement for the next three dramatic "beats."

Measure 20. Carmen looks at Don José with an expression of smug
pride; the chorus is singing about her lover.

Measure 24. Don José realizes that Escamillo is Carmen's true love.
We see it in his eyes, expression, and body language.

Figure 7 (continued). Bizet — Excerpt from *Carmen* (Act IV).

> **Measure 30.** Carmen sees that Don José now fully understands about Escamillo and that perhaps she has pushed his patience too far. She sees that he is both furious and desperate.
>
> **Measure 36.** She tries to exit again, this time knowing that if he is desperate, he might become violent. José rushes up and grabs her wrist. *He has almost two full measures of the new tempo before his musical entrance, but due to the cross rhythms and lack of*

Figure 7 (continued). Bizet — Excerpt from *Carmen* (Act IV).

clarity in the orchestral accompaniment, he will need to catch the conductor's beat.

Measure 38. He spins her around to face him (as before).

Measure 39. As she faces him, he grabs her other wrist (as before).

Measure 41. She struggles, pulling backward.

Measure 42. He pulls her up close to his face; she tries to avoid his stare. *In avoiding his stare, she can either turn downstage to draw his*

Figure 7 (continued). Bizet — Excerpt from *Carmen* (Act IV).

> *gaze forward to the audience, or she might choose to face the other way because she does not need to sing.*

Measure 46. Carmen struggles and manages to pull away, making José fall to the floor (perhaps to his knees) in the process. *More triplets against duplets ("laisse moi") illustrate her frustration with being captured by José.*

6

Figure 7 (continued). Bizet — Excerpt from *Carmen* (Act IV).

Measure 48. He reaches up and grabs her skirt as she tries to leave. *During this act, the gypsy girls usually wear traditional Spanish costume, including a lacy headdress, and each carries a fan.*

Measure 52. She pulls the skirt away and turns to confront the sprawled José — she feels empowered once more, as he lies there at her feet. *Again, she can make eye contact with the maestro as she stands still above Don José at the fortissimo tremolando.*

Measure 54. Tauntingly, she repeats that she does indeed love Escamillo. She patronizes him with the phrase "je répéterai."

5. OBSERVATIONS AND EXPLANATIONS

This example is perhaps excessively detailed, and more closely resembles the level of explanation required when working with student singers than in professional opera. It shows the breakdown of dramatic phrases (sometimes called "beats") quite clearly, however. In addition to the considerable moving around that the actors need to accomplish while singing, it includes references to their expressions and some indications as to the motivation behind the stage movement. Often it is directly driven by the text (as #54 uses the repetition of her declaration as a form of taunting), but it can also be linked with the musical material. The sounds from the *banda interna* and offstage chorus allow the stage action to come to a halt as Carmen and Don José stop to listen. This helps intensify the moments of action, much like a measure's rest of G.P. can alter musical tension. The offstage music also allows for the director to add to the dramatic material given to him in the libretto. While this example uses the musical "soundtrack" to show José's realization of Carmen's love for Escamillo, it could have been used in a variety of other ways such as a fight sequence, or perhaps some chorus members rushing across the stage as they arrive late for the bullfight.

Of course, not all scenes are like this, and not all directors require this level of attention to detail (though some prefer more). But several facts still remain about this small section of music. First, it is important that both Carmen and Don José pay attention to the directorial detail, not just for their own characters but also to learn about the approach that their colleague will take in creating the role. If nothing else, it ensures the physical safety of the singers during conflict or fight sequences. The assistant director will be taking copious notes to ensure that the director's vision and details of the blocking are recorded for later rehearsals. Similarly, the coach accompanist should pay attention to these details, so that they can support the singers as they rehearse any difficult blocking during the initial staging process. If the director has told Don José that he is psychopathically deranged by the end of the opera (rather than driven by envy, lust, love, or despair), it will alter the way that the actor creates the role, which will in turn alter some of the timbral elements of the vocal production. If the coach accompanist can incorporate the director's vision of dramatic structure into their coaching, they may become an indispensable addition to the production team.

5

THE ART OF AUDITIONING

SOME MIGHT QUESTION WHY A book on coaching should include a chapter aimed at singers. The answer is simple: Coaches are often asked for advice and opinions about this part of the singing profession. The more points they have to consider, the better their advice will be.

For singers, getting a job involves auditioning. Some people consider this as just something to endure, never considering the difficulty and complexities of the art of auditioning. In the following paragraphs, I will write some things that fly against tradition but are all based on rather sensible consideration of problems that everyone acknowledges but which few solve.

1. ACCOMPANISTS AND READING MUSIC AT SIGHT

In preparing for auditions, few singers consider the fact that the accompanist or coach will be sight-reading music, hopefully with some musicality and perception. Any number of pieces are absolutely standard repertoire, and every coach should know them. But there are far more pieces that any given coach may not know. Therefore taking a difficult Rachmaninoff song into an audition (without prior arrangement with the accompanist) is probably not a good idea. Stephen Sondheim's musicals are very popular, and it might be thought to be a good idea, when auditioning for music theater, to take his works along. The assumption is false, because his tessitura, for women in particular, is quite low (thus not showing the voice well), and the accompaniments are sometimes quite nasty. Besides, producers and directors prefer to hear songs that show the voice well and not the latest and most over-sung works.

A simple rule of thumb is this: If the singer cannot musically read the music at sight, singing only one line, he or she should not expect the coach to be able to do so. Any aria from Donizetti might be possi-ble, or Verdi or Gounod, but even there some arias will be unfamiliar. Consider the cabaletta in *Lucia di Lammermoor* to Lucia's act 1 aria: "Quando rapito in estasi." What is written and what is sung are quite different, both due to the usual interpolations and due to the sudden (unwritten) tempo changes. Coaches should know this aria, but even if they do it is always hoped that a little rehearsal will clear the interpre-tative ideas up. If no rehearsal time is available, a score marked clearly will help the coach and singer get through the aria.

On the other hand, it is always possible that a coach can play even a difficult piece at sight. I recently read the "Honor Monologue" from Verdi's *Falstaff* in an audition, and, although I had not played it in over 20 years, the piece is so logical and wonderful that it sticks to the coach's fingers and mind like honey.

2. PREPARING THE MUSIC

It used to be necessary to take huge piles of scores to auditions. This is no longer a fact of life. With a few exceptions, those running auditions do not mind photocopies, because they know that singers are using pho-tocopies as a matter of convenience. In this way, a singer can prepare a three-ringed notebook (probably with ¾-inch rings) with just the appli-cable arias in it, and he or she will not have to be thumbing through page after page of an anthology trying to find the chosen excerpt.

If real books are used, it is quite important that Post-it® notes are used to mark the pages. They stick, but they do not leave a residue. It is a forbidden sin to spend anxious moments thumbing through a score trying to find the correct pages while the accompanist and those run-ning the auditions wait.

In preparing the audition notebook, you can let pages lie flat and be marked with all manner of cuts, interpretative notes, and even tempo indications. You can even leave out omitted pages. Metronome numbers are quite handy, and most coaches can get fairly close to those numbers.

Make certain that the complete music has been copied. It is quite difficult to accompany a musical line that consists of only an occasional stem (the note heads being about an inch above the top of the page). It is equally impossible to invent the bottom notes when the left hand is omitted. On copy machines, understanding how to use the reduction capabilities will save many an audition. Usually something between 94 percent down to 85 percent will take care of all arias. While it may be wonderful to mark vocal things on the music during voice lessons, the singer should see to it that the accompanist has a clean copy, with the markings added being only those pertaining to their musical execution of the piano reduction.

If the singer sings an aria in two versions, cut and complete, put two copies of the aria in place. Installation of the music in this binder needs a little defensive discussion as well, and a coach can explain it easily to a singer. Many singers put their music in three-ring binders with each page of music being on the right-hand side, the left side being only the back of the photocopy. This means that the coach must turn after every page of music. It also means that the coach has to eliminate some of the accompaniment, and in a work like *Gretchen am Spinnrade* by Schubert, this is nonsense. Taping the music back to back or copying in duplex mode will make turning pages much simpler. Then the singer can punch the holes and insert the pages into the binder. The singer should also keep a supply of gummed reinforcing rings on hand, because they will be needed. In arias of three or four pages, it is even possible to make pages that fold out, eliminating the need for any page turns.

Another method for inserting pages in the book is by using plastic sleeves. There are coaches who disagree with this method, finding the sleeves to be difficult to turn and too glossy, but of equal importance is the fact that this preserves the music a little better, and markings can be made almost as easily on the music. Though difficult to find, plastic sleeves in matte finish are definitely preferable. The shiny sleeves, though they are fine for keeping 8 x 10 glossy photographs, are quite reflective of light and, depending on the layout of the audition room vis-à-vis a light source, can make visibility of the music impossible. If glossy is all that can be found, the coach can deal with it.

The singer should label each aria completely enough for the coach to find that next selection without the singer going back to the pianist's side. This is usually done with a tab on the outside rim of the paper, with the title carefully written on the paper tab. The coach can read the title and turn to it easily.

3. ENTERING — THE PERFORMANCE

Many directors have said that the audition begins at the entrance. The way a singer carries him or herself and acts in this difficult situation tells the director a lot about the way the singer will react in rehearsal and performance situations. The director takes in the "costume" of the auditioner (how they are dressed) and notices mannerisms, if any, that might bear watching for the next few minutes.

Most auditions are conducted with a grand piano centerstage. Even if the auditions are being held in a room of some size, the piano is most frequently in the center of the "performing" space (in classrooms this is the lecture space). The singer will want to stand in the crook of the piano to sing the number. This does not mean standing five feet in front of the piano, nor does it mean standing somewhere nearer the end of the piano. The crook of the piano is where the piano bends, where the front of the lid is flipped back. This puts the singer in their "set" and makes them look like they are performing.

Performing is what auditioning is all about. The singer must always consider the audition process as yet another venue for performing. It should not be considered as a time for thinking, "Please love me!" It *should* be taken as a time for singing and enjoying the art and act of singing. "Here I am. Enjoy my abilities. If you like me, hire me, but I'm going to enjoy performing for you at my very best for today." The singer should also take this as a cue to be as musical and insightful as he or she can be. Even though auditioning does not take place before a paying audience, the most successful auditions are those that treat the moment as if it were. "Express, don't impress" is a very good rule to go by.

Sometimes an audition will be held in a space where the piano is not centerstage. It may be farther upstage, or it may be an upright over at the edge of the stage. This may be for convenience, or it may be because the setting on the stage does not allow for a piano to be wheeled into the space. In such cases the singer will have to find the optimum space to sing, usually indicated by stronger lighting downstage center. This is, in acting terms, called "finding the light" and it may show the director some valuable insights into the singer as to how they handle this distraction and to their knowledge of stage savvy.

Assuming the piano is centerstage, how does the singer get to the pianist to give him or her the music and then swing around into the crook? This depends first on the placement of the entrance door. If the entrance is somewhere to stage left of the pianist, whether from just offstage left or from somewhere in front of the stage, the singer frequently proceeds on the downstage side of the piano, turns his or her back on those running the auditions, places the music in front of the pianist, and gives instructions. This method of entrance keeps the singer always in full view of those hearing the auditions. It also means that, while giving instructions, the back of the singer is facing to the auditors for up to 30 seconds or even more. This is not a very good idea.

Recently it has seemed to me to be a better solution to proceed on the upstage side of the piano to the area just upstage of the accompanist. This means that the lower body is somewhat out of sight for a brief time, but it means that the pile of music is placed out of view on the upstage side of the accompanist. The back is thus never to the auditors (not the best side of the singer). The singer can give the accompanist instructions as to tempi, cuts, and so on, without awkwardly having his or her backside showing. Then, when the singer comes around to the crook of the piano, he or she can see the auditors, the auditioning space, and possibly where distractions are. When entering from stage right, the goal is the same … go to the upstage side of the accompanist.

The journey to the crook of the piano is then done through a simple walk around the back of the accompanist (looking up, not down at the feet), and going into the crook of the piano — ***never turning his or her back on the auditors***, but keeping face forward while stepping into the crook area. The singer is now ready to announce his or her number.

A word should be inserted here about giving instructions to the accompanist. Any cuts should be clearly marked (see Chapter 1 for the best methods for this). Scribbling out the unused music is sloppy and negates the possibility of ever opening the cut. Again, if two versions are sometimes sung, include both copies in the folder. Some singers are even using computers to scan the music, make cuts, and put in important markings.

It is a good idea to put metronome numbers at the top of the music. Even if the composer has given them, they may not be quite what the singer wants. If a section picks up in tempo, indicate the new metronome number there as well.

Singing lightly the first phrase of the vocal line is also a very good idea to set the tempo. The vocal muscles of the singer know the speed quite well. The singer should *not* sing the accompaniment, nor should they conduct. Though many singers think of themselves as conductors, few actually are, and they may actually (read into that usually!) give the wrong tempo.

Any tempo deviation, whether accelerando, affrettando, ritardando, or whatever, should be noted. The easiest way is to put a horizontal squiggle of the duration of the ritardando. If the tempo is to increase, a straight line with an arrowhead indicating a faster tempo can also lead up to a vertical line indicating the end of the tempo fluctuation. Some-times drawing in the famous little indication of glasses will be sufficient to let the accompanist know that he or she must watch for surprises. If a printed indication is to be ignored (and many are), it is a good idea to scratch out the marking not being followed.

If embellishments are being made or cadenzas added, an indication of exactly what is being done is always quite helpful. It will ensure that the accompanist will not jump ahead of the singer or plow ahead and not listen.

Pianists are sight-reading, and the more a singer can help them do that, the more secure the audition results will be.

4. SINGING THE PIECE

Unless told otherwise beforehand, the first thing a singer will do is introduce themselves and the piece. Only introduce the first piece unless told otherwise. It may sound silly, but it is a good idea to practice this part of the audition, too. It is amazing how many singers stumble over their own names and the names of the pieces they are singing.

The following is an approximation of really bad announcing:

> "My name is JohnDoe,andIwillsing"Chegelidamanina"from*La Bohème*byPuccini."

The run-on introduction is quite unclear. Equally unclear is the following:

> "My name is John Doe, and I will sing "Che gelida manina" from La Boheme by Puccini."

These mistakes are unfortunately not at all uncommon. The first flies by so quickly that the auditors have no idea what the person has said. They are still trying to figure out who is singing, and the accompanist is already striking the A♭. The second makes the auditors think something has happened to their ears. Speaking is an integral part of many operas, and clear speaking in an audition tests that ability, too. Even in auditions for college entrance, singers need to speak clearly.

The title of the piece, unless it has a given nickname — "Musetta's Waltz," the "Toreador Song" — should be announced in the language in which it is being sung. The opera should also be announced in the correct language of the performance. For example, if a singer is sing-ing Onegin's aria, the title should be either *Eugene Onegin* or *Yevghenyi*

Onegin, depending on whether it is sung in English or Russian. (And note that some auditions require arias to be sung in *only* the original language and key.)

Acting in auditions is dependent on the kind of audition being sung. Certainly collegiate auditions should not include falling down as if in death or even leaning on the edge of the piano dramatically. Still some "attitude" is quite appropriate to project certain characters, such as Musetta or Zerbinetta.

Terribly long arias, like Zerbinetta's "Gross' mächtige Prinzessin" from Richard Strauss's *Ariadne auf Naxos*, should probably not be programmed. If they are and the auditor asks for the piece, it would be good to offer only part of it. In the case of the Strauss, the last half is universally preferred.

Once the introduction is complete, the singer can take a moment to collect their thoughts. It is not necessary then to look over to the accompanist and to nod furiously in order to get them to play. The pianist is glancing at the music, making mental notes about where to be careful, noting one more time the presence of cuts, and getting into the mood of the piece, too. They will be watching quite closely to see when the singer is ready. Even after the singer looks up confidently in an indication that they are ready to sing, it may still take a moment or two for the pianist to play that first note.

In the audition situation, a singer should realize that there are good and bad accompanists. Some accompanists seem to know exactly what the singer will do even before the singer has figured it out. They will support, follow, anticipate, and sight-read music beyond the singer's wildest imagination. Unfortunately, there are also accompanists with lesser accomplishments. They may be excellent players but may not be able to follow and read at the same time. They may not be able to absorb the chromatic additions of Fauré at sight. They may stumble over even the easiest passagework, leaving the singer with a feeling something akin to being left standing alone in the center of the arena and surrounded by lions.

The coach's job is to become as good at the audition process as they can be. The good audition accompanist is rare, and yet there is no reason for that to be the case. Mental preparation and knowledge of repertoire make the job not so terribly difficult as the lack of good accompanists might indicate. The wider the repertoire at the accompanist's beck and call, the less he or she has to absorb instantly. It is of course also the singer's job to rehearse with the coach if possible, or, barring the possibility of that, warn him or her of impending hurdles.

The singer will help this (and improve his or her auditions immeasurably) by singing the music clearly. This means not only good diction, but it also implies clear rhythms, accurate counting, observance of rests, and even knowing the music perfectly. The clearer they are about musical things, the better the coach can follow their intentions.

Even the best accompanist will make mistakes on occasion. The variables are such that it is bound to happen. It may even be a fatigue factor. The accompanist may have played a complete run-through of an opera or a full recital the night before. Earlier singers may have taxed the mental capacities for sight-reading to the limit. Whatever the problem, the singer should acknowledge no mistakes, neither the accompanist's nor their own.

The singer who sings confidently and acknowledges no mistakes will convey the content of his or her musical ideas with far greater precision, while the one who lets every slight imperfection bother them is never really "in" the piece and conveys none of the emotional intensity of the composition. (Listen to some of those opera recordings where the singers had little or no experience with singing their roles in the theater — some were made with the singer practically sight-singing — and you will hear every note in place but little musical understanding, no innate phrasing that comes with real knowledge and involvement in the proceedings. What price perfection!)

Showing mistakes to the auditor only lets them know that the singer knew they made a mistake. It really is better not to telegraph that information, since it is just possible that the auditor did not notice.

No singer should ever expect an accompanist to transpose a piece at sight. If the music cannot be found in the proper key, then it should not be programmed. Most arias should be sung only in the original key, the exceptions being some arias that are "always" transposed such as "La calunnia" from *Il Barbiere di Siviglia* by Rossini (usually sung in C major instead of D). Traditionally transposed arias exist in print in the transposed keys, so expecting the coach to transpose them at sight is not an option.

Showing any rancor when an accompanist makes a mistake is not a good idea either. If the mistakes are serious, those listening will know quite well and need no magnifying gesture from the singer. It just might also be possible that the accompanist has a say in casting or collegiate admission, and pointing up their inadequacies will not set well with him or her.

The singer should proceed as if the music is emerging perfectly. If a tempo is wrong and the accompanist immovable, the singer must either deal with it by taking the accompanist's wrong view, or they can stop and graciously suggest that they, the singer, must have given the wrong tempo. "I'm sorry, but today I seem to need a slower/faster tempo and I gave you the wrong one. Could we take it a little slower/faster?"

In such circumstances, thanking the accompanist may take great strength, but the singer must get used to the idea of doing just that. It makes the singer seem gracious and professional, and it puts a positive spin on the end of the audition. Besides, the accompanist may have made a mistake while trying to cover up an equally huge mistake made by the singer. The singer is sometimes oblivious to the dropped verse or the embellishment not taken; they may be totally unaware how many curves they threw the struggling accompanist. The gracious "thank you" heals all wounds.

The singer should remain "in the piece" throughout the entire piece, and this includes introductions, interludes, and postludes. While it is a good idea to shorten some of those lengthy pieces, it is not possible to take out all such music. Zerlina's "Vedrai, carino" has a lengthy postlude of seventeen measures that can easily be shortened to roughly three. But some singers assume that the only important time for them to be "with" the music is during their singing. This assumption is false.

I once played for two auditions back to back for the role of Susanna in *Figaro*. The singers both sang "Deh vieni non tardar." The first one gave a perfunctory reading of the recitative and actually put on an act of being bored during the introduction to the aria proper (it can't be shortened!). The singing of the aria was not bad, but the mood had been shattered, the audition lost long before that.

The second singer was clearly "in the garden" before the slight introduction to the recitative was halfway through, and she made the most of the aria introduction by looking around and absorbing the night air (which she "felt" even if we could not). At the end, she capped the audition by leaving an artificial rose on a chair. As a general rule it may not be a good idea to use props, but this once it was mightily effective. She was in the garden and absorbing the moment for all to understand. She got the role.

This ending moment can be just as important as the singing. Whether in audition or in recital, it is important to stay with the piece to its completion, and this may actually mean a second or two beyond the last vibration of the piano.

5. ANSWERING QUESTIONS

After singing the first selection, the singer can relax and gather his or her energy. The auditor will be writing thoughts down and perusing the résumé for questions he or she may want to ask. This is not a nervous time but a release time, a time when the singer can let the first piece go and get mentally cleared for the next one.

The auditor may ask any number of questions. It is the singer's job to answer as completely and as clearly as possible. It does not mean that they should volunteer reams of information beyond the parameters of the question, but the simplest answer might not give enough information either. Here is a brief exchange of questions and answers, given first with wrong answers and second with helpful answers. (And the singer must never answer with: "It's in the résumé." If it were clearly in the résumé, the auditor would probably not ask!)

Version 1:

Auditor: Very nice. Do you happen to know the other aria?

Singer: Other aria?

Auditor: The other aria that character sings in the same opera!

Singer: Oh, that. No.

Auditor: What else do you have in your repertoire?

Singer: What?

Auditor: What repertoire have you been studying?

Singer: Mozart, Rossini, Brahms, and Donizetti. A little French stuff.

Auditor: And do you dance?

Singer: No.

Auditor: What else do you have with you?

Singer: Oh, I don't know, uh, … I guess I could sing the Gounod.

Auditor: No, that isn't what I need to hear. Well, I think actually that I have heard enough. Thank you.

Version 2:

Auditor: Very nice. Do you happen to know the other aria?

Singer: I am studying it, but it is not quite ready for performance today.

Auditor: I see. What else do you have in your repertoire?

Singer: I've been studying the arias from *Don Giovanni* and *Cosi fan Tutte* by Mozart. I've been looking at the *Barber of Seville* aria. I have worked on the aria from *Lucia di Lammermoor*. I've been preparing a set of Brahms lieder for a recital next month. And I have some Reynaldo Hahn mélodies for that same recital.

Auditor: Where is that recital?

Singer: At my old college. I'm returning as an alum to sing for them.

Auditor: That's a nice idea. Do you happen to dance?

Singer: I've had only a little formal training, but I tap-danced in the show *Anything Goes* in high school. I have studied and I'm good at ballroom dancing.

Auditor: That's quite helpful. What else do you have with you?

Singer: I have brought with me the aria from Gounod's *Faust* and the aria from Massenet's *Manon*.

Auditor: Let's hear the Gounod.

(after the Gounod)

Auditor: Thank you.

Singer: Thank you. (*Gathers up music and leaves confidently*)

In the good exchange above, it is important that the singer has mentioned an upcoming recital. Even though it is a return to a college, it is a "gig," and it doesn't matter to the auditor whether it is a paid performance or not, it is a performance for which preparation is being made. The singer is working in the profession in some capacity.

6. SECOND SELECTION — PROGRAMMING THE AUDITION

The second selection to be sung may be selected by the singer or by the auditor. It depends on the venue and the way things are done. The singer must always present a printed list of possible selections (called a repertoire sheet), and the second selection is chosen from that list. The singer may even plan to sing one piece and, on the day of the audition, change to a different selection. College entrance auditions usually ask for two or three selections of the singer's choosing, but professional auditions may require much more, including a range of languages and styles. (Those printed repertoire sheets are becoming more and more the norm.)

The singer should realize that which pieces are placed on the list can make or break an audition. The pieces should normally be from one *Fach* and not cross over into odd territory. It may be very showy for a soprano to sing Isolde and the Queen of the Night (it has been done!), but it is an ultimately futile idea because it only confuses the listener. Even programming a nearby *Fach* can be dangerous. For example a soprano may be able to sing Zerbinetta (*Ariadne auf Naxos*) and Anne Trulove (*The Rake's Progress*), but the physical/vocal demands from both are so extreme that neither makes a good "curtain raiser" to the other, and it is almost certain that, if they are both written down, the singer will be asked to sing the other one second.

Even closer might be "Lohengrin's Narrative" ("Im fernen Land") and Faust's "Salut demeure," and a singer might very well be able to sing both easily. But if the tenor programs the Wagner first, he will most probably put too much weight in the climax and have nothing left for the Gounod. Programming therefore means both what pieces and what order they are sung. If the singer does not want to sing a lighter/higher piece after a heavier/lower one, program something else or sing the lighter one first.

The second piece is usually chosen to show something different from the first. This may be language, style, or fioritura. A soprano able to sing "Tu che le vanità" from *Don Carlo* should be able to sing "Ernani involami" from *Ernani* just as well, but the earlier Verdi has much more fioritura (passagework) and trips up many otherwise good Verdian sopranos. If it is given as a possibility, it will be picked, because most people know how difficult the aria is. (This actually happened at a Metropolitan Opera District Audition — the soprano sang *Don Carlo* beautifully and *Ernani* with considerably more effort.) The total package must be presented in the best way the singer can.

7. EXIT — REACTIONS FOR THE SINGER

It is possible that a singer may be asked more questions after the second piece. He or she may even be asked for a third selection. The singer should take time going into this piece, gathering up his or her thoughts and vocally remaining strength. No one should rush the singer. If those running the auditions ask for a third piece, they are interested, and the singer should let them wait a moment.

If they are not asked for a third selection (or even a second), it means nothing. As the last note of the piece fades, they should stand quietly until dismissed. It may take a few moments for those hearing the auditions to talk among themselves about the relative merits of the audition. The singer will usually be dismissed with a simple, "Thank you." As mentioned above, this requires no comment from the singer other than a reciprocal "Thank you."

Then the singer gathers up the music and walks positively from the stage. This exit (on the downstage side of the piano) can be just as important as the entrance. The singer should thank the accompanist and show absolutely no reaction to their own singing, whether that means "Hooray, I nailed that high note" or "I really sang like a pig today." Some reaction may involuntarily escape, and that can be endearing, but generally it is a good idea not to show emotions about the performance just passed.

I was once told of an actual audition that ended in the following way. It shows how important answering confidently and clearly can be.

Auditor: Thank you.

Singer: I guess I know what that means. (*Starts to leave.*)

Auditor: Wait a minute. What does that mean?

Singer: It means I don't get the job, of course.

Auditor: No, it means the audition is over. That's all "thank you" means. There is not much other way to end an audition except with "thank you." What you just said means you don't get the job. Your audition had put you in the "maybe" file. But, if you don't have confidence in your audition and ability, neither do I.

We all have auditions that are wonderful, auditions that go better than we could ever imagine, and then again there are those days we would like to crawl into a hole and forget the entire thing ever happened. The singer who is human, warm, and agreeable is always ahead of the game. If the singer shows class all the way through the audition, everyone will know.

Occasionally something happens in auditions that can be so totally unexpected that the singer must react and think on his or her feet. This can be a negative reaction to a chosen selection, a noisy cell phone call in the middle of the audition, or a personal, sexual advance toward the singer. The last is a classless thing for the auditor to do, but that has not stopped some famous directors from doing just that. The singer should be as positive as he or she can be in any situation, defending his or her choice of music ("It fits my voice, and the opera is being done a lot lately"), and defending themselves however they might — including using bold-faced lies — to get away from the director. It might be a ploy to see how much integrity the singer has, but it might also be just a crass affront. The singer must not be rude (if they want the job), but compromising themselves might not secure the desired position/role.

The coach needs to understand these things and prepare the singer for various eventualities. You just never know what will happen in the audition process. During the actual audition process, the coach/accompanist must try to be as supportive as possible, and this may just include running musical and personal interference. The odd, thoughtless, and personal rudeness of the auditors, while not defensible, is just one more variable in the audition process. No wonder singers dread the process. The positive attitude will help ward off negative problems.

I will include here a brief word about audition dress for singers. Men have it easy: They should wear a suit (blazer and slacks are fine), dress shirt and tie (turtle neck shirts are also acceptable). A pocket handkerchief is okay, too, but no visible body piercings (except maybe a small earring). Women should wear a "party" dress, meaning something that is dressy but not too formal. Women may wear some jewelry. Men and women should be prepared to wear street makeup, particularly if the audition venue is a large stage. Stage lights can make faces fade away. Blonds frequently need to darken their eyebrows slightly. The auditor needs to be able to see the face, but it must not look grotesque either. Moderation is a good thing.

8. THE COACH AS AUDITIONER

Coaches have to get jobs, too, and that means playing for conductors and producers. Conductors will want the coach to follow them, and they will also want to test their knowledge of standard repertoire. Preparing various selections ranging from Mozart to Puccini is not too taxing. But the coach should know that there are some famous audition excerpts for coaches. As mentioned in the chapter on Strauss, the act 3 opening of *Rosenkavalier* is infamous for its difficulty. Equally well known is the "Juden Chor" in *Salome*, also by Strauss. In that example, it is expected that a coach will play the piano and sing a chosen part (as they would have to do in a coaching where that part was not covered). The "Basket Scene" in Verdi's *Falstaff* is also a difficult challenge. But most auditions deal with standard repertoire.

The conductor will also be listening for interpretative ideas, good and bad. In the Toreador's aria (from *Carmen*), it is not a good idea to "interpret" the swaggering rhythm in the accompaniment, but it is better to play it straight. In these auditions, it is important that the coach has also studied the orchestral score at least enough to know why a piece needs to go one way and not another.

Realize that coaches need to know the basic repertoire more than the isolated speciality. The Metropolitan Opera once hired a coach because he could simultaneously sing and play *Lulu* by Berg. It is a difficult and challenging work to play, and it was entering their repertoire. The coach was impressive in his ability to do that task. Unfortunately, after that season he was let go because he didn't know works like *L'Elisir d'amore* or *Rigoletto*.

INTERLUDE TWO

DEALING WITH THE DIVA/DIVO

Into the lives of every coach must step the high-strung diva (female) or divo (male), and they can be extremely difficult people with whom to work. Telltale signs of being a diva/o are the phrases "I know that already," or the equally telling "I prefer to do it this way." When they begin correcting your languages, then you know you have an ego standing before you (unless you need to bone up on your languages!).

Very strong-minded singers who are not divas or divos exist, of course, and they can express (or argue) their points with equally strong convictions. But the true diva or divo takes her or his opinions and desires for expression as the only way, sometimes in the face of very strong reasons why such ideas are not viable. Their ideas frequently have a ring of unmusicality about them. The problem is sometimes not so much the ideas but the dogmatic way they choose to enforce them over even the most cogent reasons for proving them wrong.

The point of coaching is to instruct a singer in the correct ways of the music. Correct means, in this case, stylistic, dramatic, and musical accuracy and shape. So when they choose their own course or emulate their favorite recording rather than take the coach's suggestions, the coach must decide how to deal with it. The problem may involve something as basic as when to hold a high note (or not), whether in fact to sing a high note (that does not stem from the composer's pen), or even the basic tempo itself. The fact that someone has done a passage in one fashion on a recording is not a terribly valid argument for its being correct, merely that there is precedence for doing it that way.

The first problem arises usually when there is a desire to show off a particular note, but the composer has given such an accompaniment that holding it becomes impossible. It sometimes takes great determination and patience to explain the reasons why a note cannot, with any taste, be elongated. This same patience must be employed in dealing with the desire to add the unwritten notes. Traditions must be met, of course, but singers are not always as adept at singing the added notes as they presume that they are, and a coach must be tactful (but sometimes quite firm) in finding other options that are in order.

An example of the "correct" tempo can even arise in an aria as familiar as Liù's "Tu, che di gel sei cinta" (from Puccini's *Turandot*). Even well-schooled coaches love to stretch the basic tempo of the aria out to something much slower than Puccini's marking. This affords no room for the stylistically correct expansion at the high notes or dramatic phrases. A singer must be made aware of not only the correct tempo but the reason why it is correct (and the metronome number itself may not be enough of a reason for some people).

Conversely, in Gounod the coach may have to stress that Gounod's metronome numbers are almost universally too slow. No one will ever sing Marguerite's Jewel Song (from *Faust*) at the tempo he indicates. The Marguerite would die and so would the music. On the other hand, it is good to realize that a slightly slower than "usual" tempo affords the singer the possibility of singing the repeated "Réponds, réponds, réponds vite" without a drastic ritardando.

Another important possibility in handling the diva/o is to dive into the language and its implications. This will include the stage directions (in their original languages if possible). This makes the singer realize that they must work and not throw attitude. If Verdi uses the term "un fil di voce," the coach must find out if the singer understands what that means. (Literally, it means "one strand of voice.") And they must discuss how to achieve this.

In the aforementioned aria of Liù, the weighty importance of her using the word "Tu" with a Princess must be explained. Few sopranos will have considered that fine point. In using the informal form for "you," Liù is stripping away the distance between Princess and slave and is addressing Turandot woman to woman.

It is usually easiest to deal with the diva/o by taking a no-nonsense approach to what goes on in the coaching and by showing them that their attitude, so carefully constructed around their persona, does not faze the coach in the least. Flattery is wonderful in its place, and compliments should be used when work is truly good. But the coach who does nothing but pass out the compliments is serving neither the singer nor himself very well. Most singers, even those in question, want to learn the music correctly, and they will respect the coach all the more for being honest and thorough. They are paying good money for exactly that. Empty platitudes are not helpful. If the singer does not wish to follow the coach's advice, and the coach's point was valid, then the coach can always refuse future dealings with that singer.

The diva or divo who persists in retaining his or her attitudes around directors and producers will quickly find they are not hired again, so the coach will not have to deal with them much later anyway. But it can be helpful to let a singer know that his or her attitudes will not cut muster with others either.

Italian opera houses have always had prima donnas ... and primo uomos, and seconda donnas and secondo uomos. It is historically part of the Italian opera house structure. But the slang version of that position is a diva/o and might just as well be referred to as a prima donkey, for they are just as headstrong and stubborn and frequently know even less than that animal.

Why these attitudes exist can stem from any number of factors. Perhaps a singer is vocally ill at ease and having problems with a role, vocally, emotionally, or dramatically. The coach, in taking the no-nonsense approach, can actually get through the "defense" and get to the real heart of the problems. It is for that reason that coaches must consider in each coaching how to get at problems, and how to ignore the image the singer tries so hard to maintain. It may make working relationships difficult, but it may also just make the singer realize that the coach, who deals with the attitudes, is the best friend he or she can have outside of a vocal teacher. Polishing a rough musical gem into a sparkling creation takes time and talent from both singer and coach.

2

Considerations

This part will deal with specific aspects of style and other problems that arise in particular operas from certain countries and composers.

INTERLUDE THREE

COMPARING COMPOSER STYLES

Many chapters in this book compare various vocal styles with another, in a sense pitting composer against composer. What makes each composer individual? Every coach must decide these things for themselves and must codify the things that are acceptable in the work of one composer and forbidden in another.

For a good example of this, one might compare Wagner with Puccini. The slight sob in the voice, quite appropriate in works of Puccini, would seem out of place and stylistically incongruous emanating from a Wagnerian hero. Conversely, an acting style that might suggest the grand gods and goddesses of Wagner would be quite wrong for the realistic characters in Puccini.

Similarly, a metronomic pace might be perfect for an ensemble from a Mozartian opera, but a similar steadiness in Richard Strauss would kill the beauty of the work. Strauss himself said that a tempo marking is really only good for four or five measures at best.

The main differences are usually found in the way each composer treats the setting of words. In the chapter on Mussorgsky and Russian opera, we will find that the pacing of the music depends heavily on the dramatic pacing of the words. Sometimes what seems as though it should musically proceed at a steady pace will require breaks, all dependent on the flow of the words.

In preparing a score, a coach must know traditions and languages, but he must also understand the different ways in which each composer treats diacritical markings, dynamics, ritardandi, and the like. If Puccini neglects to write *a tempo* (as he frequently does in *Tosca*), it does not mean that he expects one ritardando to increase on the last one. If so, the music would come to a complete standstill. For these things coaches must use every tool possible to get at the truth: recordings, source books, tradition books.

Even composers of seemingly equal style have major differences. Salieri and Mozart would seem to be quite similar but are not. Due to the strange way Salieri cadences (as compared to Mozart's impeccable sense of musical punctuation), the recitatives written by Salieri are much more difficult to bring off than Mozart's. A coach expecting to work in exactly the same way with any two similar composers will find himself facing those differences within minutes.

Another consideration is found in the harmonic differences between different generations of composers. Singers today are not attuned to the meaning indicated by the chromatics of Mozart. Due to constant exposure to the harmonic language of Wagner, Berg, Britten, and others, singers are not aware of the importance of Mozart's chromatics. A simple look at the end of the Sextet in Mozart's *Don Giovanni* will show how chromatic Elvira is compared to the other characters. Her character is truly in anguish, trying to stand alone against their force, while the others are merely angry or haughty. Singers of Elvira are usually struggling to cut through the textures and are not thinking about the anguished line Mozart has given them. Each phrase is also twice as long as those sung by other characters. When they are made aware, they begin to understand the nature of the ensemble and character much more.

In the famous "Là ci darem la mano" duet, Zerlina's infamous chromatics as she wavers, not being "forte" enough to withstand Don Giovanni's advances, tell reams about her character. (They also sometimes tell reams about the intonation of the singer.)

A well-sung portamento is quite acceptable in Puccini. He even asks for it, as do Rossini, Verdi, and Bellini. But Mozart almost never asks for such things, and to place one within a phrase frequently seems just as out of place as an unwritten ritardando.

The hardest thing for a coach is to keep the differences of composers in his mind and to keep looking at music with fresh eyes. Things we all overlook, either through too much familiarity or through musical saturation from other styles, are frequently things the composer considered quite important. This is true as well of fermatas, both those printed on notes and those written (or implied) on rests. In *Rigoletto*, for example, in the famous aria "Cortigiani, vil razza dannata," Verdi gives Rigoletto the words "Tu taci?" He follows this with a fermata and then the sighed "Ahime!" But few baritones take the time to allow Marullo *not* to answer the question, "You're silent?" They plough ahead into the vocally resplendent "Ahime," but they inflect it with only some of the pathos it needs, because they took no fermata. This is something Mozart would not have done and which Puccini would have made more obvious. Such comparisons are essential in coaching.

6

BAROQUE OPERAS AND MOZART

IT WILL SEEM STRANGE TO some that Baroque operas and Wolfgang Amadeus Mozart are put together into one chapter. It will seem equally strange to add to that discussion the songs of Franz Schubert. But there is a method to this approach.

The early operas of Mozart are, in essence, late Baroque in style. He even inherited certain forms from Vivaldi, Scarlatti, and Handel. A frequent device found in Baroque operas was to begin and end in the same keys. Mozart did this in his operas without exception. He also used the da capo aria at times. The attention to words, though specifically treated differently by the composers in the different eras, still bears some of the same traits, and vocal techniques retained some similarities through that entire expanse of time. And the song literature will be part of any opera coach's work.

1. BAROQUE OPERA

The Baroque operas encompass a wide range of styles. In a sense, including Monteverdi and Handel in one grouping called Baroque is like putting Puccini and John Adams together today. In both cases, the composers are separated by about 100 years and share few stylistic traits.

Monteverdi is such an important composer that his operatic style needs some important discussion. Despite a prolific operatic output, only three of his operas are regularly performed today. *L'Orfeo*, *L'Incoronazione di Poppea*, and *Il Ritorno d'Ulisse in Patria* are the only surviving operas we have from him. Though they are not identical in style, they share several consistent traits. Most scenes in these operas are constructed of alternating passages of recitative and arioso. While some passages might be called monologues, there are few outright arias as we know them in the nineteenth-century sense. The recitatives must be treated somewhat freely, but with strict observance of note values. It is the tempo that alters, not the rhythm. The arioso sections frequently are in a triple rhythm or in a march rhythm. The key to these passages is found in the "swing" of the section. Monteverdi may have a lullaby (Arnalta's "Oblivion"), which rocks in a gentle two to the measure, or he may have a dance feeling almost akin to a modern (nineteenth-century) waltz.

One practice found in Monteverdi that lasted all the way through the bel canto period was the use of C to indicate recitative. Though in later years this became synonymous with 4/4 time, in recitative passages these measures have, in effect, no meter at all. They usually contain four quarter notes' worth of rhythm, but they may just as easily expand to include five, six, or more beats. This is not a mistake. In Monteverdi, for example, the measure lengths have more to do with phrasing of verbal nuances than any musical impetus.

In order to study a scene or two from Monteverdi, let us begin with the *L'Incoronazione di Poppea*. In the prologue to *Poppea*, the usually employed Overture has many hemiolas, but still is in either a majestic pace (bars 1–17) or is dancelike (bars 18–33). Leppard repeats certain sections of the Overture to give it more length, but such repeats are not absolutely necessary. It is curtain music and not a formal overture.

Fortuna begins the prologue. Her lines, snide and dismissive, are delivered with self-righteous pomposity. This means that the speed must not be too great. A slightly slower than normal speech tempo will do quite nicely. The measures should be "conducted" or felt with large beats for each half note in the measure. At the words "Dissipata, disusata," the "meter" becomes triple, moving along at a simple, flowing pace. With such syllabification, it is not necessary to be smooth. The desired effect is relatively legato, but the singer must point words up for meaning. At "Gia regina ...," the recitative returns. This pattern continues until the words "Chi professa virtù." The Naples edition of the opera calls this an aria. It is in 4/4 time and has wonderful word painting on "richezze" and "gloria," of which the singer must make use. Modest embellishments can also be inserted. The last word of her aria is her name — Fortuna. This requires some embellishment on

Figure 8   Monteverdi — *L'Incoronazione di Poppea* — Prologue — excerpt shown first as written and with two possible embellishments.

the "-tu-" syllable. In early Monteverdi, the trillo or nanny-goat trill would have been used. Some feel that *Poppea* is already at the end of this era, and a small flourish above the note might be more in order. (See Figure 8.)

Virtù answers with a tirade of her own. It is strictly recitative and includes some wonderful moments of word painting. "Sommergiti" is depicted in such a way as might indicate that Virtù drives Fortuna back. The later word "ascende" literally does that. But Virtù's entire vocal line has a different character than Fortuna. Where Fortuna was hectoring and somewhat aggressive and pushy, Virtù retains shorter phrases, seemingly indicating a stately (stodgy?) character. Note, for example, the repeated ego boost at "Io son ... io son la tramontana." She is either puffing herself up or terribly insecure. The rising vocal line indicates the former. Her greatest self-congratulatory gesture is her rise up to Olympus. As the phrases beginning "Può dirsi, senza adulazione" indicate, Virtù can be just as catty as Fortuna. Her first mention of her rival includes the vocal put-down of the flatted E, a note that is almost bluesy in nature. It is dismissive in its own right.

Amore's entrance is wonderfully impudent but also is mostly recitative. The Leppard edition gives a long flourish to underline the entrance itself. (He also transposes the role of Amore up higher in order for a light soprano to duplicate the ingenuous quality of a boy soprano, as does Curtis.) The duet reply by Virtù and Fortuna is snippy and full of sarcasm. All of this comes across only if the diction is really clear. The rhythms must be followed explicitly, but there is a flexibility of tempo not found in later Baroque. It is worth remembering here that the "inventors" of opera considered the words to be of great importance, and coloring them with scalar passages, leaps, or descending or ascending word painting was quite accepted as the way to underline the text.

An even better example of the importance of the words is found in Ottone's monologue from act I, scene XII (as numbered in the Curtis edition). Except for the recurring refrain — "Otton, Otton, torna, torna in te stesso" — the piece is entirely in recitative. The refrain, so smooth and seemingly self-indulgent, is in reality more a beginning cry for vengeance. Ottone is simply pushing himself to act, now that he has realized the true nature and danger of Poppea. The recitative of the scene is dependent on the singer's ability as an actor to convey the changing emotions of the character. His bitter pining for Poppea pushes him into extreme measures and into a great depression. The coach must work with Ottone to find the shifting moods of his character. The music follows suit, not the other way around. The coach must realize that the "metric accent" is not really applicable here, and that the bar line is basically to hold things together.

The end of the scene with Drusilla (scene XIII) is an even better indicator of this. Left alone, Ottone declaims, "Le tempeste del cor, le tempeste del cor tutte tranquilla ..." This is printed in a pattern looking like 4/4, but it sings in a triple rhythm, which lands on "cor" each time. It is in passages like this that a coach and singer must really understand Italian. As should be obvious from the above, the words are of paramount importance. This means not only diction of consonants and vowels but what I call "thought diction." If the dramatic impetus for the words does not come across, the singer has not done his job. The shifting rhythms over the 4/4 meter add greatly to Ottone's agitation. When the singers treat the text in this fashion, Monteverdi is constantly interesting ... and if not, he can be deadly boring.

In the French Baroque, the words can require even more pointing. But the French opera, in works like those of Rameau and Lully, requires a certain feel for the dance rhythms that occur as well. These are a far cry from the Italian waltz and march rhythms that invade Monteverdi. They are almost courtly or balletic in their majesty. Yet the tempos can project a wide variety of emotions and intensity. The difficulty of singing these works in the correct fashion and the scarcity of editions have kept them out of the active repertoire. This is changing somewhat. The audience, however, must be taught about this repertoire in order to appreciate it. Perhaps performances that do occur would do well to keep the drama to the fore, not slighting the correct stylistic elements, but also not creating a musical style so stilted that few modern singers or audiences will "get" it.

With the works of Scarlatti, Vivaldi, and Handel, the Italian Baroque took a new turn. (Little seems to have been done in Germany in the German language in the field of opera. At least no German opera is in the current repertoire.) The plots of many of these operas are long on complication and number of characters, while some of them are short on what we call good character development in the later nineteenth-century sense. This makes the coach's job quite difficult. Helping a singer find the basis for a character is exacerbated by the length of the operas and the — seemingly — whimsical ways of the plot. The shifting love interests in works like *Alcina* by Handel make the works confusing and hard to follow. A work like *Griselda* by Alessandro Scarlatti has some wonderful music, which is pulled down by a large number of irrelevant numbers for the secondary characters. Even a relatively strong dramatic structure like Handel's *Giulio Cesare* has moments of considerable *longueur*. In addition to the quest for a dramatic structure, though, is the need to have the singers sing with great intensity and beauty. That is the point of Baroque opera. The purity of singing must never be sacrificed to the nineteenth-century "god" of high drama. Yet high drama must be conveyed with singular intensity, an intensity conveyed through word pointing and not demonstrative "acting."

Then there are those da capo arias! Scarlatti is said to have originated these — he certainly used them extensively. The accepted dramatic idea is simple. The singer sings the A section (usually rather long, in two or three sections), then the ritornello finishes the piece in the original key. The B section follows and is relatively short (about a third the length of the A). The key for the B section is frequently the relative major or minor, or it may be a third or a fifth away. The singer may add some embellishments here, particularly in the later portion, where frequently the words from the first few phrases of the B are repeated. Then the singer returns to the A section. The dramatic revelations from the B section are supposed to affect the meaning of the A. Hence, to highlight this changed perspective, the singer embellishes the notes. It is in actuality as much a vocal embellishment as a dramatic one, but the problem for the coach and singer is to find embellishments that fit the given singer. It is appalling how many singers listen to recordings to get ideas and end up copying the ornaments sung by Renée Fleming, Beverly Sills, Joan Sutherland, or Natalie Dessay (some of questionable style). These probably will not fit their voices well at all, but the singer would rather risk a bad impression vocally than invent a set of ornaments devised for their own voices. Few if any singers today can or should even try to invent spontaneous ornamentation through "inspired" improvisation. And some famous singers admit to employing conservative solutions. It is still the drama that must be served, not just the purist's need to hear added notes.

The singing style must be expressive though not overly Romantic. The volume required for nineteenth-century repertoire is not necessary here. The theaters of the Baroque era held only 250 to 750 people, and their very intimacy (with two or three balconies) aided the singer in putting the nuances across. It is a style combining nuance and great technique in singing. The written scales, arpeggios, and cantilenas required perfect technical poise. The added embellishments make the music even harder. The good coach must be helpful yet strong-minded about the purity of singing. Due to the kind of leisurely pace and the dramatic form of the works, the modern stage director will find these works more difficult than a Shakespearean drama. The opera coach will find it no less taxing.

But how to ornament? In Figures 9, 10, and 11 the reader will find some examples of works printed with first the vocal line given, and then with an ornamented version. These are but examples. The ornaments employed can only hint at the variety possible.

Another thing the coach must keep in mind is the continuing influence of dance rhythms on arias. This was the music of the time, and it was most popular, so composers were sure to employ it. The lift and buoyancy of rhythms found in dance will help the coach (and conductor) find the path to a proper style for the Baroque. Since dancers do not slow down, neither (usually) should a sung tempo. Once set a tempo should proceed along at a very steady pace, not yielding to the singer's penchant for holding notes or expanding phrases. The chosen tempo needs to reflect the difficulty of the most elaborate passages. The "more

Figure 9 Handel — *Alcina* M excerpt.

Figure 10   Handel — *Alcina* M #22.

expressive" way of singing is perfect in Romantic music or possibly even in music of the Classical era, but it is not correct in Baroque. Only the final cadences are traditionally expanded a little. Even there moderation is the key. Moderation is a key to the added cadenzas in some arias as well. (The highly emotional, adagio arias of some of the Baroque operas can embrace some slight elongations of rests for expressive reasons. But in these instances, the composers clearly indicate the possibility for this by interrupting the constant rhythm in the accompaniment.)

Some passagework, within a steady tempo, may have some "inégale" sixteenth notes. Stressing the first note of a group of four sixteenths not only helps the singers know where they are, but it also gives shape to the passage, making it flexible and beautiful rather than a machine on automatic. The tenuto first note must not be too long, but must be elongated just enough to give that shape.

Similarly, it is in the Baroque era that the problem mentioned in an earlier chapter appears most frequently — that of writing rhythms of similar passages differently. Printed in Chapter 3 (Figure 6a) is a passage from Handel's *Alcina*, written first as it is printed and second as it might be performed. Technically, the changed rhythm might be

Figure 11 Handel — *Alcina* M #23.

considered an embellishment, but there are conductors who consider that Handel actually intended both passages, orchestral and vocal, to be performed in the same rhythm.

One wonderfully confusing passage in Figure 12 comes from a number Scarlatti actually cut from *Griselda*. The written rhythms seem really strange, but playing them erases the problems at once and shows that they should be performed in the second fashion.

One important facet of Baroque playing and singing is a specific embellishment of rapid decrescendo. The embellishment has been given a name by members of Apollo's Fire, the Cleveland Baroque Orchestra. Jeannette Sorrell, its music director, says that they call this embellishment a "whale tone." With apologies to the leviathans of the deep, it has nothing to do with them except for their physical shape. Drawing a shape of a whale facing left (with no tail fins!) gives a perfect image of the shape of the longish note. A "soft" attack followed by

Figure 12 (a) A. Scarlatti — *Griselda* — as it is printed. (b) Scarlatti — as it should be played.

a quick but long decrescendo creates a separation quite light and flexible, without great effort for the singers.

Since coaches will be asked (or forced) to coach oratorios of this era, a few words are necessary in this area as well. It is generally accepted that the natural flow and freedom one finds in the Mozart recitatives (to be discussed later) is somewhat more restrictive in Italian Baroque opera (though the difference is not as great as some scholars might make one believe). But oratorio is even more restrictive. The recitatives are short and usually are sung with more emotional weight than that found in operas. They carry also the weight of symbolism. The "halo" around the voice of Christ in the Passions comes from the sustained strings. (One other symbol of this "halo" is found in the fact that strings — made of gut, or flesh — are stretched across a wooden bridge.

The symbolism of flesh across wood *is* a Baroque way of thinking.) The voices usually retain all correct rhythms and a relatively slow tempo. Bach Passions have some solos that are inordinately difficult to sing. Each Evangelist passage, for example, is written high and exposed, the recitatives sitting quite high for the tenor's projection of text.

There are, of course, the secular cantatas of Bach. Any good performance of Bach's *Coffee Cantata* or Telemann's *Canary Cantata* must bring out the humor inherent in those delightful works. The woman's insouciant need for coffee — "Coffee muss ich haben" — "I must have coffee" — is a far cry from the arias of the St. Matthew. Yet attention to shape and words is just as important.

2. MOZART

All of these styles require a good voice and technique. Mozart is, however, the composer from this era who speaks to the most of those born in the twentieth century. His operas are, even in the early works, filled with personality, and the characters act naturally. The reactions they show may be those of a character caught off-guard, or they may be filtered through courtly manners and mannerisms. But how astute of Mozart to give us the flesh and blood of Don Giovanni, Leporello, the Count and Countess, Figaro and Susanna, Osmin, Papageno, Tamino, the Queen of the Night, and a whole roster of others. Each shows flashes of real humanity, nobility, foolishness, pride, and evil residing side by side.

Vocalization in Mozart (as in the Baroque) requires careful dynamic shading. It also demands a purity of vocal line — full and clear but never forced. It is tempting for a singer performing the Count in *Figaro*, for example, to explode various words in his recitative and aria "Hai già vinta la causa." But the moment "Perfidi" explodes out of the vocal line, the singer sounds stylistically out of place. Verdi and Puccini do not allow for such moments of excess either, but they do not seem quite so out of place with them as with Mozart. The portamento appropriate in the later composers is equally out of place in Mozart's works.

Mozart recitatives are amazingly facile and natural. The chapter on recitatives applies perhaps most to his style of writing. No less an authority than conductor Riccardo Muti has expressed his astonishment on Mozart's writing of recitatives. He has said that the harmonic shifts, cadences, and shaping of vocal lines in recitatives are so apt that they become uncanny. This makes the argument that Mozart did not write the recitatives for *La Clemenza di Tito* all the more cogent, since they are of a quality inferior to the bulk of his works. Those recitatives seem awkwardly phrased and flow badly from moment to moment. Even the recitatives (usually jettisoned) in his first opera, *Bastien und Bastienne*, are well written. (Mozart only wrote part of the opera with recitatives, and then stopped. Perhaps this was when he decided that German should not be used in secco recitatives.) Mozart occasionally indulges in the "incorrect" accent just to be more expressive. Again, it is vitally important for a coach to listen carefully, or a singer might just sing "dunQUE" or "senZA" and make a shambles of a subtlety or verbal rhythm.

(I might just mention here that Mozart's direct contemporary Salieri requires a much different approach. While one can say his music is just inferior to Mozart's, the real fact is that it is simply different. And the recitatives don't cadence in nearly the same brilliant and logical fashion found in Mozart. His musical numbers also show real form and poise, but not the secure invention Mozart shows in every page.)

But it is in the musical numbers that a coach must take the most care. Particularly in the ensembles, it is necessary to have not only the notes together, but the words as well, balanced so that each strand of voice and text comes through clearly. Each consonant must "pop" at the same time as the next singer's. The act 2 trio and finale from *Le Nozze di Figaro* or the great Sextet in *Don Giovanni* show these problems quite well. Poised, modulated singing as a unit must carry the day. The singers, who, even for a moment, try to out-sing each other in a work like the "Farewell" trio from act 1 of *Così fan tutte* will sound loud and ungraceful. In the comic effect of having Fiordiligi and Dorabella slightly try to outdo each other, the effect must not be too overt, or it becomes ugly. The coach's job is to balance such ensembles, vocally, dramatically, and musically.

In Mozart the generally accepted range of tempi has expanded in recent years (usually to the faster). The coach must have a good idea of the usual tempi and a passing understanding of the newer trends. Portamentos, cadential ritardandos, and held notes are just not in place in Mozart's musical fabric. The coach will sometimes have to have a firm idea of good Mozart style and enforce it.

Due to the range of accepted tempi, a good method for rehearsing arias and ensembles (duets, trios, etc.) is to take a slightly different tempo every rehearsal. This keeps the singers flexible. When the conductor arrives, they can set the tempi and give the shape they desire for the pieces. Always bear in mind that some conductors take extreme tempi, both slow and fast, and it would be wise to point out to singers some indication of what the "norm" is. A friend of mine gave me a listing of metronome numbers taken by singers and conductors in various recordings of "Ach, ich fuhl's." The range was mostly from 48 up to 72 for an eighth note. One recording, Roger Norrington's, took 106 to the eighth! You really never know for certain what tempo to expect.

During coaching sessions, some discussion may be necessary to make singers aware of the implications of exactly what they are singing. To generations brought up on Wagner, Berg, Stravinsky, and Schönberg, Mozart's brief excursions into chromatics can fly by unnoticed. But to Mozart, a moment of chromaticism is important. He was brought up on Baroque examples, where even a half-step might carry dramatic significance. Consider the duet "Là ci darem la mano" from *Don Giovanni.* When Zerlina wavers in her resolve, Mozart gives her a progression in descending half-steps. It brings out her indecision quite well (and is seldom in tune).

Chromatics are not the only point with implications. Today an aria like "Vedrai, carino" (also for Zerlina and from *Don Giovanni*) seems innocuous enough. Yet the delicate and sensual insouciance of the piece is quite bold for the late eighteenth century. The subject matter, always tastefully handled of course, borders on the personal and very private. How else to "cure" Masetto's ills. But few sopranos realize the boldness of the concept. It may not greatly affect the way they sing the aria, but an awareness of this is important nonetheless.

Some of Mozart's musical numbers are predictable, being based on the Baroque models. For example, "Dove sono" from *Figaro* is at first a da capo aria, then breaks off entering into a section that looks forward to the bel canto era form known as a cabaletta. Many arias have similar structures. The more formal ones include the recitativo accompagnato at the beginning. But some numbers take on larger forms. These are based on an almost symphonic structure. Arias like "Martern aller Arten" from *Die Entführung aus dem Serail* or "Parto, parto" from *La Clemenza di Tito* are quite large in scope, having multiple sections and tempi. These must be musically organized in coaching sessions, so that the singer understands where the piece is going.

The symphonic background of Mozart helps hold his larger operas together in other ways, too. Trios, like the one from act 1 of *Figaro* or from act 2 of *Idomeneo,* are all built around nonvocal forms. The music seems to dictate the drama unfolding rather than formal considerations. How else to explain numbers like the second act Finale from *Figaro*? These symphonic movements bring up a controversial point in Mozart's writing: the presence of tempo relationships.

A tempo relationship can be defined as two sections of music that have differing tempo indications, but which have some relationship between basic pulses. A prime example would be the first three sections of that second act Finale from *Figaro* mentioned above. The *allegro* that launches the Finale is in a headlong rush and in cut time. The half note equals approximately 90 beats per minute. This section continues up to the moment when Susanna steps gingerly (and impudently) from the "gabinetto" as a Cherubino replacement (usurping his B♭ key as well). A case could be made that the pulse of the minuet section continues at 90, but that the beat switches to eighths. As the Count enters the gabinetto, the tempo changes again, returning to the original tempo. This continues all the way up to Figaro's entrance, where a totally new section, scene, and tempo occur.

Another obvious tempo relationship occurs in Sesto's "Parto, parto" from *La Clemenza di Tito*. Here the faster section must be twice as fast as the first. Mozart proves this by bringing back music from the first section, written in double the note values. Since the music can't proceed at two totally different tempi, the second tempo has to be related to the first. The coda seems not to be related to either previous tempo.

A case might be made that whole scenes in Mozart's operas, including separate numbers, are related. If all the numbers from the first scene of *Don Giovanni*, for example, were taken at tempi chosen with an ear for these relationships, the unit of the scene might be felt. This sounds, on paper at least, as if a conductor might be trying to straitjacket things into a preconceived mold, but that's not the case. "Ideal" tempi vary from production to production, and these tempo relationships might actually seem within the realm of possibility. More clearly this means that all of the following numbers (and sections) would have some pulse relationships: Leporello's opening muttering to himself ("Notte e giorno") — pulse in half notes, the furious pursuit of Donna Anna (without the usual accelerando at the entrance), the sword fight, the Commendatore's death — pulse in quarter notes, and the body of the vengeance duet — pulse again in halfs. A new pulse begins at the scene change and Donna Elvira's entrance. Some of these tempi might seem too fast or too slow if such relationships are held rigorously, but the possibility still exists that they were intended and the idea is put forward only for serious consideration, as some people believe quite strongly in the theory.

Despite even the existence of the most obvious numbers like "Parto, parto," some esteemed musical experts insist that tempo relationships do not exist, feeling that this binds all musicians. Whether a conductor or coach wants to follow these relationships or not is unimportant; it is still a valid point of discussion. And to ignore them on principle is, to quote Meredith Willson's *The Music Man*, "closing your eyes to a situation you do not wish to acknowledge!"

Another question that needs to be discussed in a Mozartian context is whether or not to ornament Mozart's music. The current vogue is to add ornamentation to the vocal line as in Baroque operas. Earlier conductors of the 1930s through the 1960s would have shuddered at this suggestion, some of them even eschewing appoggiaturas. It is clear, particularly in the *opera serie* of Mozart, that cadenzas at final cadences were expected. This discussion is not, however, about the occasional appoggiatura or cadenza. It is about the actual changing of the vocal line by adding passing tones and other such devices. While these are perfectly in line with Baroque practice, and they recur in the bel canto era, Mozart's music does not seem to need such changes. But it is also a valid argument that ornamentation did not simply drop off the face of the earth during Mozart's time. When a conductor asks a singer to ornament an aria that is already as difficult as "Or sai chi l'onore" from *Don Giovanni*, then one should start to question the whole ideal of such changes. For a coach, the best advice would be to add things only in extreme moderation. A little graceful addition in something like "Se vuol ballare" might be appropriate. But asking Despina to sing "Una donna" with the violin figures instead of her own much clearer notes (measures 39 through 44 — "voglio farsi ubbidir, e qual regina col posso e voglio farsi ubbidir") flies in the face of Mozart's genius. It actually appears on a recording (unnamed here)!

Mozart also requires vocalism free of unwanted portamentos. A few are possible, usually in emotional phrases like the Countess's "Fa—mmi or cercar, da una mia serva aita" (*Figaro*). But sloppy vocalism in Mozart is as unforgiving as faulty intonation. Mozart robbed the singer of these liberties simply by writing the way he did.

One point about alteration does require comment, however. In several operas, Mozart seems to have written with minor (and some major) inconsistencies. The orchestra will play a figure dotted, and the singer or singers will answer with no dots. There can be no single answer to this problem. Instead, one must study each measure and decide for that moment. An example can be found in the first phrase of Don Ottavio's "Il mio tesoro." The orchestra has a dotted figure, but when the singer answers his words "mio tesoro" are not supposed to be dotted. Some conductors find this to be a glaring and obvious error. Others argue strongly that "tesoro" means "treasure" and that tossing away the first syllable of "tesoro" too glibly flies in the face of the meaning. Again, each case will be different.

Similarly in *Don Giovanni*, act 1 finale, the orchestra clearly dots its fanfares, but Don Giovanni (and the others after him) sing "Viva la liberta!" without dots. Can this be right? The decision must be made by the conductor as to how strictly he wants to follow what is written.

Così fan tutte is quite another case altogether. The score shows many instances of being written in haste, two of which are given here. In the Sextet, mm. 38 and following (Dover/Peters publication), Ferrando and Don Alfonso are shown singing as a pair, while Guglielmo sings a different rhythm below. This does not make a whole lot of musical or dramatic sense. Many people switch the baritones, allowing Don Alfonso to answer alone, while the two young men are paired.

The other example of "haste makes trouble" appears in the Duetto between Dorabella and Guglielmo. Dorabella's vocal line is "shadowed" by the first violins from measure 9 through measure 15, with only one or two pitches not played. But in measure 13, the last thirty-second note is different. This makes no sense. The NMA changes one to coincide with the other, but did they have to make a decision? It is illogical that the two notes should coexist! The score has many more examples too numerous to confront for the restricted space here.

Mozart could organize his operas with amazing tonal security. Studying the tonal outline of *Figaro*, for example, shows repetitions of keys, pairing of tonalities, and indeed an order of key progression not experienced in any of his later works. And some keys even take on a sort of "identity" for a character (Cherubino and his "substitutes" are frequently in B♭).

In his later operas, Mozart began simplifying his musical forms. *La Clemenza di Tito* has many numbers that are formally less complicated. The nature of the music seems quite easy, but upon study the singer will find it requires considerable vocal poise. This simplicity is a key to the later Mozart. It makes the larger numbers for Sesto and Vitellia even more impressive. The duets between Annio and Servillia or Annio and Sesto are simple. Their textures are much less contrapuntal. The music here also sounds like a close cousin to the opera written simultaneously with it: *Die Zauberflöte*. The textures allow words to come across with much greater clarity and emotion. Such simplicity occurs first perhaps in the "Farewell" trio in *Così fan tutte*. There the simplicity is akin to the songs Mozart wrote, and his songs lead to Schubert.

Opera coaches are required to coach song literature, too, at times, particularly if they are in scholastic institutions or in private practice. Opera singers need to prepare song recitals, too, and they frequently lean on their opera coaches for this.

Schubert songs are not opera, and singers should not sing most of them as if they were. His songs require a restrained rendition, with heightened awareness of verbal nuance and drama. Where arias exist on a larger dramatic beat (possibly no more than two or three "dramatic beats" per aria), a song can change such "beats" quickly. This is done with far more coloration of the voice and dramatic underpinning of the text. One must not forget, however, that Schubert is the Romantic Classicist. He is "Classical" but leans toward the Romantic spirit.

Some of his songs are dramas all by themselves. "Gretchen am Spinnrade" is a whole monologue, a solo drama, written out with every nuance given to the voice, but with every click and whir of the spinning wheel clearly audible. In the piano accompaniment no pedal is necessary until the portion where Gretchen becomes dreamy, thinking fondly of Faust's stately bearing and manners. "Erlkönig" is no less vivid. But these are overt, early lieder. Even "Auf dem Wasser zu singen" carries its own kind of drama. And full-throated singing, which successfully conveys the emotion of Romantic arias, must be tempered with a much wider dynamic palette.

Schumann or Brahms are much more Romantic in their approaches to lieder. They allow more overt drama to come out, sometimes reveling in the self-pity of their poems. Schumann's Heine settings convey the bitter outbursts and harsh irony of forsaken love to its fullest. But in his restrained and Classical way, Schubert harks back vocally to the earlier composers covered in this chapter. There is unfortunately no way to cover all of the lieder composers and their differences in this volume.

In passing to the next chapter, it bears noting here that Beethoven and Weber operas require a singing similar in clean lines and form to Mozart, but they additionally require more vocal heft. They also point the way to the Richards, Wagner and Strauss.

INTERLUDE FOUR

THE ISSUE OF STRAIGHT TONES

The most controversial vocal question of the Baroque and Mozartian era is that of singing with what is called "straight tone." Straight tone is, as the name would imply, singing with no vibrato. Such singing is used at times in nineteenth-century lieder and twentieth-century opera to indicate emotions ranging from weary to deranged. It is sometimes called for with indications like "tonlos" (literally "without tone"). A perfect place for such a coloration would be in the beginning of the Schumann lied "Ich hab im Traum geweinet" ("I've wept in my dreams"), from *Dichterliebe*. There the world-weary, lovelorn singer is in deepest despair, and straight tone conveys this easily.

It is unfortunate that we have no recordings of singers of the eighteenth century, and few composers wrote about the voices per se. There are statements about the abilities of various singers, frequently to the detrimental side, but the quality of the voices is almost never described. Mozart wrote, for example, about the Ferrarese sisters (originators of the sister roles in *Così fan tutte*) and about those who originated the roles of Idomeneo and Osmin. But only in the latter is there some mention of tonal quality.

The Baroque treatises make mention of a kind of embellishment in which the singer starts a tone with no vibrato and adds the vibrato as a coloration device. Some modern musicologists and conductors have taken this to mean that the normal singing style was without vibrato. But the ornament is used today in popular music, too. Frank Sinatra used the emotive "embellishment" in songs like "New York, New York," starting those long, last notes with a straight tone and adding vibrato to increase the dynamic rendering.

The truth is that singing without vibrato means either that the singer is "holding" the tone straight or else is using no support. With intricate vocal passages such as those given to Bradamante and Ruggiero in *Alcina* by Handel, "holding" the tone makes such fast passages impossible. If diaphragmatic support is not used, the passages will lack clarity and projection. A singer of Bradamante could never penetrate the textures of the orchestra in her aria "Vorrei vendicarmi" if she is not supporting her voice well.

The question of support has even come into question by some who believe that the "modern" support was a thing unknown in Handel's time. Vocal writing in *Alcina, Giulio Cesare*, and many other Handel operas shows that some support had to be used. Besides that, the operas of Mozart were less than fifty years ahead, and arias like "Come scoglio" or "Hai già vinta la causa!" cannot be sung without very good support and vocal technique.

The Manuel Garcia family, father and son particularly, who were active in Rossini's time, taught voice and began the scientific study of voice production, but it is certain that they did not invent it. Good vocal technique was established before they came along. Their vocal teachings indicate that a well-supported tone has a freedom to it, with a light vibrato warming the sounds produced. This vibrato adds to the spin and projection of a vocal tone.

This modest vibrato is not to be confused with the rapid tremolo that inflicts some singers today, nor can the style of vocal production required in Baroque opera be equated with the "tutta forza" (full force) singing found in Verdi or with the long, sustained lines found in Wagner and Strauss.

Choral singing in Baroque times must just as surely have included this kind of easy vibrato as did the solo singing. Choruses today, when asked to sing with a totally straight tone, tend to sound flat in pitch, shallow and colorless. While this can be a wonderful effect, it severely limits their vocal appeal. A straight tone will hinder the choral rendering of fast passages (such as the chorus "And he shall purify" from Handel's *Messiah*) as much as a vibrato-ridden one will.

Some solo singers still perform coloratura passages in a sketchy fashion, slipping over the notes without really sounding them cleanly. If this is the only way singing with straight tone can produce the passages, then it is further evidence that such singing cannot be authentic. Straight tone is not necessary to achieve intonation in choral singing. Verdi and Wagner choruses must be sung with the same attention to intonation as a Bach, Handel, or Scarlatti chorus.

Another question in singing, related to straight tone, is the question of what constitutes singing in tune. Pianos, harpsichords, and most organs are tuned in equal temperament so that they can play comfortably in any tonality. Some organs are tuned however in different tuning scales, so that the pure thirds sound clearly in D major or C major, but they sound quite odd indeed when D♭ major or B major is attempted. One of the joys of orchestras is that they can tune to the various keys in which they play, moving the thirds wider or narrower to make the correct tonality sound out cleanly. Indeed, this is one of the main differences between well-trained orchestras and the student orchestras found at the high school level. Singers also adjust naturally to sing in any given key. Equal temperament is not innate with singers. The "ring" of the barbershop quartet is achieved by just this intentional adjusting, and they, too, sing with a very modest vibrato, at times taking their tones straight in order to increase the "ring."

It must be admitted that orchestras in Baroque and Classical times played with no vibrato, or at least far less, than they do today. This comes from the treatises on string playing published by various teachers along the way (including Leopold Mozart). But it does not necessarily transfer completely to solo singing. It might just be that it was felt that vibrato would get in the way of fast string passages (as it does in rapid vocal passages). But the beautiful lines heard in string writing from Baroque and Classical pieces for orchestra may have also been expected to receive the warming influence of an easy vibrato just as surely as it was expected in vocal writing. (It might be a point to ponder that the straight tone in orchestras was employed because keeping the chamber orchestras in tune back then made the cleanest tone possible a necessity.) Woodwinds and brass in ensembles do not usually play with vibrato even today, but their pitch is more fixed than that of strings.

In orchestral writing considerable points for debate arise concerning the use of straight tone or not. But to those who understand vocal production, consistent singing with a straight tone is considered a mistake, based on misinformation, antiquated thinking, and a lack of the knowledge of what constituted good singing back in Handel's time.

An important point to all coaches would be that volume is not the goal in Baroque singing (or in most Mozart). Colorful usage of the language (usually Italian) plus well-modulated (with a good dynamic

7

THE BEL CANTO MOVEMENT

GIOACCHINO ANTONIO ROSSINI, GAETANO DONIZETTI, and Vincenzo Bellini are the three composers most associated with what is called the *bel canto* era. Bel canto means, literally, beautiful singing. This means more than just producing a nice vocal tone, however. It involves the coloring of words, the embellishing of vocal lines, and a purity of vocal production peculiar to that age and to these composers. The three are linked so closely because, although there are great stylistic differences between each of them, they were all born within ten years of one another.

Difficulties found in Rossini's operas stem from three things: coloratura, speedy patter, and the seemingly endless energy of the music. The vocal lines are almost instrumental in their structure. A violinist could play Cinderella's last Rondeau with just as much flair and virtuosity and sound more idiomatic doing so. But Rossini writes for singers, and there are many singers today who can sing the scales, trills, arpeggios, and other roulades with almost frightening ease. It seems the trouble in the coloratura comes not so much in the execution of the notes but in the learning of them. When a singer learns any passagework incorrectly, it takes a long time to unlearn the mistakes. The coach must carefully help the singer to learn the right notes. Grouping notes into patterns helps the singer grasp the concept of the passage. Then the singer must learn to phrase the passagework so that it does not come out as mechanical note-by-note articulation. Such musicality is extremely important because, without it, the music has no beauty.

Patter is another matter entirely. Figaro, Dandini, and indeed whole casts must learn passages that fly by verbally with great speed. Consider the act 1 aria of Doctor Bartolo in *Il Barbiere di Siviglia*. The aria "A un dottor della mia sorte" begins simply enough. But beginning with the *allegro vivace*, the difficulty of performing speed steps to the fore. The Bartolo cannot begin singing "Signorina, un altra volta ... " up to speed. The only way to learn such passages is to write the words down (with all repeats), and then, while walking to work, doing laundry, or other such mundane things, say the text clearly over and over, gradually increasing the speed. Muscle memory must be brought into play here. The physical act of producing the words is what must be learned. The words also come too fast to think much about the meaning. The bass-baritone must know the meaning and project as much of it as he can, but the sheer physical act of singing the words is quite difficult. Besides, it can be argued that Rossini wrote, as he sometimes did, with a verbal effect in mind. Bartolo splutters and splutters, but we, the audience, want to know that the singer is really singing the words and not just faking them. (This same technique is useful when dealing with Gilbert and Sullivan patter songs.) It is important for the coach to realize that these passages must be sung absolutely in time, without rubato. That is the only way to get the rhythmic precision into any passage. But not every syllable is equally important. Consequently, the only way for an audience to get "every" word is to allow some syllables to be softer. In that way the important words and syllables come through, but the precision remains.

A very famous example from *Pirates of Penzance* by Gilbert and Sullivan will serve to demonstrate what I mean more easily than an Italian text:

I AM the very MOdel of a MODern major GENeral

I've INformation VEgetable, ANimal and MIneral ...

This will sound out to the audience much more clearly than singing every syllable with equal weight and importance.

Clean singing is imperative in Rossini due to the boundless energy his music seems to have. When a passage is really cleanly sung or played, it seems much faster than it may in fact be. The final stretta in the act 1 finale of *Barbiere* shows this quite well. When all the dotted rhythms dance along together, and when the triplets fly from the orchestra, the whole piece seems light and full of energy. If any one element is lacking, the whole thing just gets heavier, and a faster tempo only muddies the problem. And a tempo that is too slow will kill the piece almost as soon as it kills the singers.

Rossini could also write beautiful cantilenas, but they are not his normal milieu. "Lyric" for Rossini is usually typified by something akin to the "Cujus animam" in the *Stabat Mater*. Truly lyric music, like the soprano's "Sombre forêt (Selva opaca)" in *Guillaume Tell*, is quite special and just as difficult to limn well as any Rondeau from the earlier operas. One problem these lyric movements call up is the necessity of finding places to breathe. Sometimes the easiest place musically is impossible because the word does not break there. The coach must be adept at finding the best places.

In Rossini's comic operas, the recitatives chortle along more rapidly than Mozart's usually do. He seldom pauses to let a point sink in. But there are many traditional additions, both dramatically and musically, which are made. This usually involves acting through the dramatically awkward moments. Added pauses, hesitations, chuckles, and the like are all traditions. To learn these, the coach must resort to studying a variety of sources like Ricci, recordings, and older coaches. Some of them are actually printed in the back of some scores. The director or conductor will add others. Though the recitatives can stand handsomely as written, these added interpolations are quite within the spirit of the libretto, and they add immensely to the audience's enjoyment and understanding of what is going on.

Rossini, more than perhaps any other bel canto composer, requires some embellishments. These are almost all codified in the Ricci book mentioned elsewhere in this volume, but many can also be found in other publications. The embellishments may vary, but they remain surprisingly limited to a traditional few. Sopranos and mezzo-sopranos do far more embellishing than tenors, baritones, or basses. Men cannot usually move their voices fast enough for many alterations of the notes. Their changes usually consist of added higher notes. The more a coach can know about these changes without always looking them up, the better. No singer should expect to improvise the embellishments, however. One suspects that, even in the Baroque era, possible embellishments were worked out in advance. According to Richard Bonynge (in an interview during a Metropolitan Opera broadcast), that was certainly the case with the embellishments used by his wife, Joan Sutherland. He was never sure exactly which embellishments she would use in any given performance. Most artists find it necessary to know exactly what notes they plan to use. Those who wait, expecting some divine spirit to guide them, end up obviously wavering and unsure in performance, with conductors trying to follow them. Opera is not a game of chance.

Another aspect of Rossini is what is called the Rossini Crescendo, aspects of which can be heard even in his first opera, *La Cambiale di Matrimonio*. The orchestra usually starts a small, motoric theme, singers scurrying along above it. Gradually new patterns are used and other singers join in. The effect can spread over several pages, but must be carefully rehearsed to make certain that the effect does not get out of hand, with the volume going too loud too soon. (Donizetti and Verdi had their own way of dealing with this kind of ensemble and crescendo, and those also must be carefully rehearsed.)

Despite being a bel canto composer, Vincenzo Bellini has a much different musical style to coach from Rossini or Donizetti. For his operas, the cantilena is paramount. Think only of the incredible beauty of "O quante volte" from *I Capuleti e i Montecchi* or "Casta diva" from *Norma* and one knows immediately where the extreme difficulty lies. Such legato singing is quite difficult to achieve, and any imperfection in the technique shows immediately.

Bellini is compared with Chopin with good reason. The melodies have a similarity of arch and poise. And the fioritura that glides from the fingers or throat during those melodies is of a similar chromaticism, extension, and grace. These flights of fancy (for such they must seem) are difficult to negotiate, and a coach will have to have some knowledge of voice and vocalism to help singers learn how to traverse these passages with ease. As with Mozart and Rossini, Bellini's melodies and fioratura show off any faulty intonation or technique immediately.

Bellini, as with Chopin, seems to call for great elasticity in tempo. But after comparing performances where such facile shifts of tempo are the norm with those in which a more Beethovenian strength and rigor is employed, it becomes clear that too much pulling of tempo for every difficult piece of passagework only unravels the musical tapestry. A more Classical approach seems called for.

For a coach, however, the two most difficult problems are tempi and the intense recitatives. Some pieces from Bellini are so well known that the tempo springs to mind almost without consideration of other possibilities. But in a scene such as the first duet between Romeo and Giulietta in *I Capuleti e i Montecchi*, the tempo indication can lead any musician into tempi either too fast or too slow. Some conductors actually solve tempo problems by shifting gears in mid-movement, adjusting the tempo when the music becomes more difficult. This is done by highly reputable conductors, and perhaps it should be considered as viable. But such adjustments also tear a music fabric apart, by making too many small divisions. Finding a generally correct tempo first, one that fits all moments, then slightly pushing the tempo slower or faster seems a better option.

There are also, as with Rossini, some traditions, which have become part of the Bellini fabric. Since his operas, other than *Norma*, have become mainstream only in the last few years, these traditions are fewer and less well ensconced in our minds. One such tradition comes from the stretta to the duet "Mira, o Norma." In the second verse of "Si, fino all'ore …," at "per ricovrarci," some conductors (notably Richard Bonynge) inject a massive ritardando for about four measures. This is not written, and its inclusion seems rather willful. Neither the verbal nor musical text point to such a tempo shift. It is certainly a tradition, as it is heard in earlier recordings as well, but it should be subject to scrutiny and reconsideration, as should all traditions and embellishments. Tradition does not mean that a passage must be done exactly the same way every time.

Perhaps the greater challenge for a coach and singer, however, will come in the recitatives. Even in his lighter operas, such as *La Sonnambula*, Bellini has an ability to instill his recitatives with great intensity. He does not allow his singers to toss off lines simply, as do Rossini and Donizetti. Almost every line carries with it some depth of feeling. This is even more true in *Norma*, where the subject matter involves jealousy, the possibility of Norma killing her children, and revenge. Bellini expects the singers to be able to invest lines like "Oh, rimembranza!" ("Oh, remembrance") with great emotion, whether elation or depression.

Gaetano Donizetti is perhaps the easiest of the three to bring to life. His recitatives sing so naturally, and he captures subtle shades of meaning almost as well as Bellini. Donizetti has a less artsy way of composing than Bellini, though, and he is not as glib as Rossini. What he can be is seemingly long-winded. A study of the ensembles in *Lucia di Lammermoor* or *L'Elisir d'amore* reveals ensembles that build beautifully from small solo lines to tutti outbursts. The trouble is that they sometimes go on for a rather long time. The great stretta after the sextet in *Lucia di Lammermoor*, for example, dramatically sounds wonderful, with shifting tonalities here and there surprising us and making us perk up. But onstage the drawn swords are not striking anything. They're waving ineffectively in midair. Everyone just stands around and sings. Though the formal need of the piece is met, the dramatic need keeps calling out to "get on with it." In Donizetti's days this may not have been as much a problem as it is today, with our overexposure to dramatic possibilities from movies and TV. It is up to the director and conductor to know how much to sing or not. The coach needs to know the traditional cuts employed when concision is desired.

Some cuts are made, too, because singers do not want to (or cannot) sing certain passages. One traditional cut in *L'Elisir* involves the cabaletta to the aria "Prendi." Adina sings the words slowly then launches into a rapid-fire passage of triplets. She is to sing this not once but twice, with Nemorino joining in on the second verse with comments about Dr. Dulcamara having been right all along (he still does not "get it"), all climaxing with the soprano and tenor singing high notes. But lyric sopranos, who might be quite successful elsewhere, do not always have the dexterity for such passages, so the traditional cut is made. This and various repetitive passages in ensembles involve the majority of cuts in *L'Elisir*. Donizetti himself supplied some "ossia" passages to eliminate some of the more difficult coloratura, should the soprano need it. Some of the traditional cuts, however, are questionable. To cut two bars here and four there just to make things easier does not make much sense to a conscientious musician. Yet those and some very much larger ones occur, whole scenes or numbers being skipped over lightly as if they were of no importance.

One other kind of cut found in that opera, and indeed in all of the operas of the bel canto era, is the kind imposed on various codas. After the main body of an aria or duet or ensemble has been sung (sometimes with only one verse instead of the two composed), the composers usually spin out the subject matter of the music to include a coda. This coda frequently has various sections, most being four- or eight-bar units. Some of these sections seem superfluous. They either beat the V–I cadence to death, or they involve coloratura passagework suddenly being thrust on singers who have sung no such passage elsewhere in the opera. A simple cut of four or eight bars simplifies the passage, but also lets it drive home more quickly to the climax. An example of this might be found in the trio from the second act of *Il Barbiere di Siviglia*. Almaviva and Rosina are being hurried along by Figaro, who is trying to get them out the window before they are discovered. But they are so happy that they begin a passage of thirty-second notes on the words "amor pietá." It seems as if they will never end. Rossini finally has Figaro abruptly change tonal center and interrupt them, urging them on. The thirty-second note passage is high and difficult (particularly for the tenor) and is frequently cut, Figaro jumping in several measures early and saving the tenor and mezzo some possible embarrassment.

In his comedies Donizetti's recitatives were originally, like Rossini's, of the secco variety. Later the harpsichord was replaced with piano. But by the 1830s, he used "secco recitativo" far more sparingly. *L'Elisir* has very few pages of secco recitativo. By 1843, his last year of composition, Donizetti leaves out the piano altogether. *Don Pasquale* uses a recitative that is *almost* secco, but the chords are played either short or long by the orchestra. Donizetti also used another kind of dialogue substitute in his operas, something he used to great effect in *Lucia di Lammermoor.*

Instead of held or sounded chords, Donizetti begins an innocuous little melody, usually in the violins, and has the singers sing parlando phrases, not usually very melodic in nature, above this. The opening of *Don Pasquale* or the passage leading up to the sextet in *Lucia di Lammermoor* are perfect examples of this.

Donizetti's melodies carry with them a stronger profile than those of either Rossini or Bellini. The conception of melody actually seems to be both fuller and simpler, pointing in many ways to the stronger tunes of Verdi. His immense appeal probably stems more from his memorable tunes than his dramatic convictions, even though these were very good. A coach must help singers keep these robust melodies fitting the best that bel canto can offer. The term "can belto" is an indication, however jokingly used, of improper force behind Donizetti's music.

One other important thing to consider is that the bel canto composers frequently give a musical signal that must be followed even when the word "ritardando" is not included. This is found in those passages where the music goes along at an even pace and then comes to a central cadence. The accompaniment stops, but the vocal line continues. The next measure may have an isolated chord or short figure and the voice continues. In a measure or two, the orchestra resumes its regular tempo. This is usually an indication that the singer, not driven along by the consistently motoric notes in the orchestra, can take some freedom. The following passage from "Largo al factotum" (*Il Barbiere di Siviglia*) shows this well. (See Figure 13.)

One caveat must be made for the three bel canto composers: Their operas exist in many bad editions. The faults range from important material being cut to inaccurate passagework, and from incorrect keys to inaccurate verbal text or faulty dynamic and articulation markings. This is more extensively covered in the appendix, but it is something of which all coaches need to be aware.

It remains to finish this chapter with a return to the words "bel canto." The expectation of the composer was that the singer, through enunciation of the text, minor vocal embellishments, well-modulated volume — extremely soft up to healthy *forte* — and, yes, a beautifully produced tone, would bring the text and music to life. In this they hark back to the Baroque era, and look forward, particularly in Donizetti, to Verdi. It might not be an exaggeration to say that the famous "silence"

Figure 13 Rossini — *Il Barbiere de Siviglia M* "Largo al factotum."

of Rossini, the period of nearly forty years before his death when he wrote no operas, might have been brought about by the change in vocal styles as much or more than the change in compositional styles. With the purity of vocal emissions giving way to the *tutta forza* singing of later Verdi, Rossini may have just opted to bow out gracefully.

Figure 13 (continued). Rossini — *Il Barbiere de Siviglia* "Largo al factotum."

INTERLUDE FIVE

"PARK AND BARK"

Before leaving bel canto and entering into Verdi, I feel we should touch on the singing style jokingly, affectionately, and accurately referred to as "park and bark." What is that?

There are moments in operas when people, usually alone onstage, stand centerstage at the footlights and sing an aria. In some productions this aria is "delivered" in an uninvolved fashion or in a generically phrased way in an attempt to please the audience in the rafters. This tends to come across as a show staged for those in the nosebleed seats, and it has minimal effect dramatically. In essence, the singer "parks" him- or herself in the most important part of the stage and "barks" the music to the rafters, which is to say he or she doesn't sing it very well. Barking of dogs has no musical line or meaning, and neither does the delivered aria.

This term can also be used for major ensembles. Even in good performances, numbers like the Sextet in *Lucia di Lammermoor* take on an aspect of "P & B." This is unavoidable in such numbers, since the whole purpose is to show that something "restrains" them from action at such a moment. Pieces like that become an exercise in outsinging in volume every other singer on the stage — if possible. Everyone can smile at this terminology, and we all recognize its presence in certain performances. But how do we counteract the negative aspects of such a performance style?

The coach is the first place that an antidote can be found. In Scenas (to be defined in the next chapter) the coach can help the singer to tear apart the text and make the most of it. This will help the singer gain specificity in the deliverance of the music and text. It will also help to mold the larger forms into a meaningful unit. Since "P & B" usually implies an avoidance of dynamics anywhere lower than mf, the coach can help to reinforce the written dynamics, thus helping the singer to find new shadings of musical expression.

The vocal teacher and coach can work on musical line, too. Over-singing usually affects a singer's ability to sustain beautiful cantilena (singing line) and both people can work with the singer to keep or to restore the line to the voice. Some of the greatest singers of the past could sing Verdi with impeccable line, and yet they had little sense of the phrasing in French music. Oddly, those singers most successful in Verdi seem ill at ease or less committed in Puccini, and vice versa.

The conductor can aid the counterattack on "P & B" by working through arias and ensembles carefully, making sure that text comes through with as much clarity as possible. They can also judge tempi to keep them from getting too fast or too slow. Singers are not always the best judge of tempo, but some conductors don't really realize the effect a tempo that is just a little extreme on either side can have.

The grander operas of the mid-nineteenth century will always have an element of "Park and Bark," but with a little care those moments will become highlights of drama and singing and not just moments to endure "crowd-pleasing" bombast.

8

VERDI

No COMPOSER CAN CLAIM TO hold a larger percentage of the operatic repertoire securely in his grasp than Giuseppe Verdi. Most of his
popularity comes from the period of composition after 1850, with each
one of these operas, *Les Vêpres Siciliennes* being the only exception,
remaining a mainstay in almost every opera house. In the last forty
years even the earlier operas of *Macbeth*, *Nabucco*, and *Luisa Miller*,
once universally ignored, have become popular and well known. And
yet the opera coach must understand how Verdi differs stylistically
from the various composers of the bel canto era. His demands vocally
are easier to understand, since we have a plethora of recordings that
ably demonstrate what good Verdi singing is all about. We even have
recordings of a few singers in the Verdi roles they originated. Since
Verdi is so popular, it only means that a coach must objectively study
the style and know exactly what those great singers are doing in order
to separate style from tradition.

Some aspects of style are bound up in tradition, but others are not.
The added high-note endings of many arias are tradition, though one
might argue that they are stylistically correct, too. Style involves the
approach to the singing itself, while traditions are answers to problems that have arisen where the music seems to call out for help —
added high notes, cuts, and so on. In Verdi, style and tradition are so
interwoven that differentiating between the two becomes difficult. The
style of singing is strongly limned, with clear diction and emotional
stances (that are not quite realistic).

Verdi's characters are all of the grand manner, larger than life and filled with intense emotions. The simpler characters found in Donizetti's *L'Elisir d'amore* or Rossini's *Il Barbiere di Siviglia* are nowhere in evidence in Verdi, for his operas include counts, Ethiopian princesses, jealous moors, consumptive courtesans, a protestant minister, a crazed gypsy, and even a hunchback. And none of them are in normal, everyday situations. These great characters demand a dramatic conviction that many singers today cannot muster easily. As befits the acting style of the day, Verdi's characters can take up poetic stances, act heroically, and fly into rages quite easily, usually with wonderfully grand gestures.

The famous drawings and descriptions of Delsarte outline the grand gestures that were used consistently then. Delsarte demonstrates a kind of codification to the kind of acting that was normal in the nineteenth century. To us in the twenty-first century, it seems artificial and overblown, but if used with total conviction, this blueprint for acting can become quite powerful and shows just how effective the combination of the gestures and the music of the era could be. We still use some of these gestures in a simplified form today. The modern gestures are usually much more restrained, but, if you take a quick listen to any Verdi opera, the word "restrained" will not, as a general rule, come to mind.

This also explains why Verdi became one of the composers to set the plays of Shakespeare to music most effectively, for Shakespeare's dramas contain emotions that are just as monumental as Verdi's music. Play actors of the time used to use those gestures and overblown ways to interpret the high emotions of Shakespeare, too. A simple listen to older recordings of actors performing some of the Shakesperean monologues will show an acting style that sounds remarkably close to operatic singing and an uncanny ability to "ham it up" in the most obvious way.[1]

One of the most prolific dramatists and librettists of the time was Eugene Scribe. Auber, Meyerbeer, and even Verdi himself used his libretti. The young Henrik Ibsen, the dramatist who almost singlehandedly changed the face of drama, was known to rail against Scribe, bothered by the preponderance of chance meetings, purloined letters, and mistaken identities.[2] These devices did not bother Verdi greatly. As long as the drama was strong and clearly set forward, those improbabilities only added to his sense of drama. His usual librettists, Piave or Cammarano, followed this mold well.

Reading Verdi's letters reveals some other aspects of his writing. He loved sharp contrasts, dynamics that go from soft to extremely loud or emotions that shift violently from one to another. A famous example comes in act 2 of *Otello*. There the Moor is listening to Iago's soothing dream — "Era la notte." Iago leads the subject back to the handkerchief as he quietly lets "drop" the words "Quel fazzoletto ieri, ... certo ne son ... lo vidi in man di Cassio" ("That handkerchief ... yesterday ... I'm pretty sure ... I saw in the hand of Cassio"). Verdi indicates that this line almost falls from Iago's lips. (Despite the crescendo many baritones employ, Verdi writes *pp, cupo* — a covered tone — and a casualness that totally disarms Otello.) Otello's reaction — "Ah! mille vite gli donasse Iddio!" ("Ah, if God had but given him a thousand lives!") — literally explodes from him. This is followed by the great duet "Si pel ciel." A coach must find the way to help a singer mold such scenes, understanding that the contrast, whether going from soft to loud or the other way around, is effective only if it is set up carefully. If Iago soothingly spins the tale of his dream correctly, Otello will be hanging on every word, and the casual (almost hissed) mention of "Cassio" will quite adequately trigger the explosion that comes.[3]

Throughout Verdi's compositional life, he made great usage of rests. In some cases, the rests can say as much about a character's state of mind as the words and the music. Many singers do not understand that, when Verdi stops the accompaniment, he is also giving the singer a license to have some freedom. Instead, many singers rush through the rests in tempo, even continuing with the singing earlier than indicated, whereas Verdi clearly expected a slight lengthening of the rests. The rests are, in dramatic terms, an indication of the pensive thoughts that lead up to the aria. The rests may be the great breath before the actual aria is launched. In any case, the coach must make the singer aware of the purpose of the rests, and then they must be worked through to ensure that the correct purpose comes out. The great artistry of a Manrico (in *Il Trovatore*) comes through not in how he holds the (unwritten) high C at the end of "Di quella pira" but in how he molds the recitative phrases, rests and all, leading into "Ah si, ben mio."

A coach must also find ways for singers to let "terrible" emotions out without hurting the voice or without their losing control. Emotive moments such as Manrico's fourth act confrontation with Leonora — "Parlar non vuoi? Balen tremendo! ... Dal mio rivalo! Intendo, intendo! Ha quest'infame l'amor venduto ..." ("You won't speak? A terrible thought! ... From my rival! I understand, I understand! This wretched woman has sold her love ...") — can bring out dangerous levels of forceful singing. A good coach can aid the singer in realizing the highest level of outburst without approaching the level where harm occurs. This is done in part by using a very focused vocal placement in preference to a wider, open-throated technique. Franco Corelli and Mario del Monaco were noted for that full *tenorial squillando* (the tenor's ability almost to cry or scream, but always on pitch and at a feverish level), but for most that kind of singing is difficult to sustain for an entire aria, let alone an entire role. Other tenors, such as Jussi Bjoerling, Carlo Bergonzi, Luciano Pavarotti, and Enrico Caruso, have used a narrower approach to the upper-middle range, the high notes relying more on "ping" than brute force. Using the verbal nuances can also help make the dramatic points without relying only on vocal heft. Diction is very important in projecting Verdian drama. Shaping musical phrases is only part of the Verdian style; the other half is shaping and enunciating the ideas that make the drama propulsive. Luciano Pavarotti has been criticized at times for "not acting," but, instead of overt acting out of emotions and situations, he lets the well-articulated text speak for him.

The vocal technique able to cope with Verdi must also possess a good sense of line. This is that kind of singing in which the notes seem to be bound inevitably to one another. It goes beyond simple legato and includes phrasing and coloration of the voice. Even those passages that might be called recitative require a stronger sense of line than similar passages in Donizetti. Though volume is not the goal per se, it is sometimes necessary to sing rather forcefully in order to project well against the orchestra or to reach the level of drama Verdi intended.

Verdi's orchestration can occasionally be very heavy, frequently an influence left from his earlier education orchestrating for a band. Trumpets are used in places where Donizetti (not one accused of scoring lightly) would never use them.

The vibrant singing voice in which vibrato plays a vital role is a necessity in Verdian singing. The kind of vibrato employed, however, must not be too wide nor must it be too quick or too slow. The vibrato bordering on tremolo is frequently considered quite unattractive. Yet a voice that takes on the heavier repertory too early will gain a slow, wide vibrato and seem worn before its time. A careful study of the few recordings of Victor Maurel and Francesco Tamagno (the original Iago/Falstaff and Otello, respectively) will show somewhat the kind of voice Verdi knew and expected. The recordings show voices that have bright focus and size, but the sensation of size comes from the bright focus, not from the pushed timbre. The opera coach will not be teaching voice to the singer, but knowledge of the voice will definitely help the coach understand just who should sing Verdi and will also deepen their ability to get the best results from a singer with minimal effort for them.

Though an opera coach does not need to understand totally what Verdi meant by "tinta," it is important for him to realize that each Verdi opera has its own musical language. Verdi referred to *tinta* as the specific color each opera needed to be a unit in and of itself. *La Traviata*, premiered only two months after *Il Trovatore*, has almost nothing in common musically with that earlier opera. The same can be said between any two Verdi operas. He inserts little musical figures that carry through a score that help to unify the piece. Look, for example, at the grace notes that appear at the beginning of the introduction to Phillip's aria, "Elle ne m'aime pas" (ossia — "Ella giammai m'amo"). The same figure appears at the very beginning of the original opening chorus and elsewhere throughout the score.

Generally Verdi has, in some sense, a compositional line directly descended from Claudio Monteverdi. His music is written with the vocal line poised above the bass line. The accompaniment never interferes with this concept, but instead it highlights it and drives it forward with a homophonic texture at once compositionally new and yet reflective of what went before. The style is of course much different from Monteverdi, but the superstructure of the opera relies on the same compositional principles. Even in the later operas, *Otello* and *Falstaff*, Verdi's more complex orchestral underpinning is related to his earlier compositional style.

Though Donizetti is also known to have taken great pains with the structure of the libretti of his operas, Verdi went so far as to dictate specific poetic kinds of verses, number of lines, and emotional framework. Reading any of his letters reveals this in depth.[4] The later the work of Verdi, the more letters can be found. Similarly, the later the opera, the longer the *Disposizione Scenica* (the detailed directorial book of the first production). Reading such letters and books can sometimes reveal what Verdi thought about the characters (and the singers!), the phrasing, and the dramatic focus. He was never one to be shy about telling the librettists what he wanted! Or singers how to sing his operas! A coach might do well to study structures of drama to aid in understanding Verdi's operas.

It would be wise here to mention the prevalent musical forms Verdi inherited from Donizetti. These forms remain in evidence even in the early Puccini operas, notably *Manon Lescaut*. The first of these forms is the *Scena*. While this means simply "Scene" in English, it has a set form a coach needs to understand and appreciate. The *Scena* begins either with a recitative or with a *tempo d'attacco* (tempo of the attack). The former is basically what was covered in an earlier chapter. The latter is a bit more musical, including moments of arioso or perhaps even full verses of music. This section is not, however, formal in structure, as it has few repetitions and does not come to a final cadence. When it does cadence, it leads directly into the next section, which is the cavatina.

The cavatina (usually an introductory aria) is slow. It may be andante, adagio, or even moderato. The form may be two verses (as in Violetta's "Ah, forse lui ...") or it may be a *romanza* (Manrico's "Ah si, ben mio"). It will always have a lyric impetus and carry an emotion that is either reflective or pleading. It may be sad or happy, but it will come to a completely clear end before proceeding to the next section.

The cavatina is followed by the *tempo di mezzo*. This is *not* when the mezzo-soprano interrupts the principal singer (although that sometimes does happen). It is the tempo of the middle and refers to the transitional section of music leading to the cabaletta. It may be recitative in nature or it may be a tempo that is consistently moving forward. It may also have several sections. But it will inevitably lead to the climactic aria: the cabaletta.

Cabaletta is an aria in two verses, fast in nature and normally heroic or vengeful. Typical examples can be found easily in *Il Trovatore, La Traviata*, and *Macbeth*. The baritone *scena* in *La Forza del Destino*, beginning at "Morir, tremenda cosa — Urna fatale del mio destino," ("To die, what an awesome thought! — Urn fatal of my destiny") leads into the cabaletta "Egli salvo." But as this has only one verse, some people say it is not a true cabaletta. It *is* of course a cabaletta, but it is reflective of Verdi's ways of remolding existing forms to his own dramatic needs.

In act 4 of *Il Trovatore*, the famous "Miserere" is actually nothing more than the tempo di mezzo between Leonora's cavatina and cabaletta (the latter frequently omitted since Verdi himself omitted it in his French version of the opera).

The ensemble form is quite similar. Taking *Aïda* as a prime example, the act 3 duet between Aïda and Radames begins with a *tempo d'attacco* with several sections: "Pur ti reveggo, mia dolce Aïda ..." ("At last I'm with you again, my sweet Aïda") is the first, while "Nel fiero anelito di nuovo guerra ..." ("Eager for fierce new battles ...") is the second. Aïda takes the third section with "Nè d'Amneris paventi il vindice furor?" ("And don't you fear the vindictive wrath of Amneris?"). The *Adagio* (as the formal section is called) begins at the *Andantino*, where Aïda sings "Fuggiam gli arbori inospiti ..." ("Let us flee from these inhospitable glades"), and leads through her statement to Radames's *risposta* (response), "Sovra una terra estrania" ("To a foreign land"). Though there *should* be a brief transition back to Aïda's music, here there is not. When she takes up her music again, Radames sings with her, muttering soft answering phrases. This *Adagio* is the equivalent of the *Scena*'s cavatina.

The *tempo di mezzo* begins when Radames sings, "Aïda!" and she answers with "Tu non m'ami ... Va!" ("You don't love me ... Go!") The *stretta* (the cabaletta of the ensemble form) begins with Radames's "Si: fuggiam da queste mura, ..." ("Yes: let us flee from these walls"). Aïda answers with the same music, and the stretta continues straight through to the moment of interruption ... "Ma dimmi ..." ("But tell me ...") Then the scene is lopped off and the dramatic coda to the act appears.

Another ensemble worthy of study for form is the Germont-Violetta duet. There the *tempo d'attacco* comprises several sections, the *Adagio* not beginning until Violetta (quite far into the scene) sings, "Dite alla giovine ..." ("Tell your daughter ..."). The *stretta*, rather obviously, begins at "Morrò" ("I'll die!").

One thing Verdi does almost better than any other composer might be called the duet as conversation. The two duet scenes from *La Traviata*, the duets of Violetta first with Alfredo and later with his father, are excellent examples of this kind of scene. The drama unfolds at a leisurely yet sustained pace. The singers must understand all of the text and color each word tellingly. They should even be made aware of the form, so they understand where they are dramatically. Some other duets are more volatile conversations, but the great difficulty in even the quietest duets is finding the inexorable drama and making it unfold. If the coach can understand this, it will help the singers immensely.

When Verdi began writing operas, his scores were not written with very many markings to indicate how a singer should sing certain lines. As he matured, he added more and more of these. A quick study of *Don Carlo*, *Aïda*, *Otello*, or *Falstaff* will show how much he began to indicate. Accents, portamentos (gentle slides from one note to another), vocal indications — such as *un fil di voce* (literally "one strand of voice") or *cupo* (covered) — and tenuto marks all become standard fare, and they are plentiful. This compositional trait was also picked up by Massenet and Puccini. The coach must help the singer realize all of these dutifully but with understanding. Once the effect is added to the notes, half of the characterization is done.

A good musical example to study for markings would be the act 1 duet between Violetta and Alfredo in *La Traviata* (this is also a perfect case for the duet form described above). When Alfredo begins his slow verse — "Un di felice eterea" ("One day happy, ethereal") — he is uncertain of himself. He has blurted out that he's loved Violetta for a year, and now he has to explain. Verdi inserts rests in the middle of the phrases in order to make Alfredo seem to consider every word. When the same music comes again, the rests are fewer, because Alfredo is warming up to his story. At the words "misterioso, misterioso altero" ("Mysterious, mysterious and aloof"), Verdi places staccato marks over the notes with a phrase marking. This marking means that the singer must gently nudge each note, not really breaking the legato momentum, but not singing smoothly either. Violetta's *risposta* is light and frivolous, in fact too frivolous. She doth protest too much. She is greatly affected by Alfredo's words.

Skipping to the *stretta* section, the backstage *banda* begins again. (Traditionally a *banda* was never orchestrated by the composer but by the local companies, depending on what they had available — the task of orchestration can frequently fall to the coach!) Violetta says, "Amor dunque non più" ("Love, no more about that"). Alfredo replies with a very curt "Io v'obbedisco." ("I will obey you.") Verdi gives Alfredo a phrase with many rests in it. This shows us that, to cover Alfredo's hurt, he becomes very formal — one can almost see him bow slightly and begin to leave. Violetta softens her point by giving Alfredo a flower, which he is to return when it has faded. Since it is an orchid/camellia (which does not last long), it means that he must return tomorrow. A coach must know that the orchestra enters part way through this section, warming up the texture and Alfredo's joyous response. In this duet a coach must understand what each mark of Verdi's means, how to sing it, and how to shape the scene as a whole. He must also know how to put together the difficult duet cadenza at the end of the slow movement. The traditions, such as ritardandi at high notes, he must either know or surmise. They must be there or the style is not right.

One point not covered yet is the tessitura in which Verdi wrote many of his roles. Whether soprano, mezzo, tenor, baritone, or bass, each role demands an ability to sing as much as a third higher than in roles so labeled in the works of the bel canto era. While some of the tessitura comes from unwritten and added high notes, even what Verdi wrote hangs in the upper fourth of the voice. This tessitura is certainly in part supposed to aid the singer in projecting the heightened emotions over the fuller Verdian orchestra. But it also means a great deal of work (and vocal wear) for the singer. (Orchestras, particularly in Europe, might do well to consider this when pitching their "A" at levels almost a half step above A–440.)

All coaches will, at some time, have to put together some of the large ensembles that are the climax of some of Verdi's operas. It is important, before the first rehearsal, to analyze them and decide how to make them not only clear but build to the important climax the composer intended. Particularly those ensembles of the later operas, like *Aïda* and *Don Carlos*, have layers of sound and shifting tempos that build to a pinnacle of sound. But these ensembles do not build themselves. While a chorus master will put together the major part of the choral work, it is up to the coach to make certain that the soloists lead the ensembles. Even major conductors have underestimated the difficulty of some of these climactic moments, and the performances have suffered because of it. The important lines must come out, each singer fitting into the whole fabric.

A coach would do well to study older recordings to learn about the cuts that they take, the cuts that Italian opera houses have usually followed. Curiously, the penchant for cutting Verdi stops around *Un Ballo in Maschera*. There, as Verdi matured and made his operas more compact, the need for cutting went away. Though a minor cut or two may still appear in *Aïda* or *Otello*, they are far fewer than those operas of the 1850s or earlier. Also, in the later operas, Verdi's sense of balance is so complete that any cut can frequently be felt much more noticeably than in the operas before 1850. *Don Carlo* is an exception to this, but it is also, uncut, almost an hour longer than *Aïda*.

It is important for a coach to understand these varying aspects of Verdi's output: arias, ensembles, and vocal requirements. When a singer wants to advance to learning the great roles Verdi wrote, a good coach must help him acquire the means to traverse the territory safely.

Verdi's musical legacy demands a brief reference to Ponchielli. His style seems at first rather close to Verdi's, and the vocal demands are similar. One might even point out that the libretto to Ponchielli's great opera *La Gioconda* was penned by Arrigo Boito (anagrammed as Tobio Gorria), librettist for Verdi's *Otello* and *Falstaff*. Also the grand manner, the overblown emotions, and the spectacle are all as much a part of Ponchielli as they are Verdi. The elaborate rubato written in by (and also added to) Puccini and the other verismo composers first appears as part of the Ponchielli musical language. His music shows a composer with many of the same techniques in place that Verdi used, and yet his musical language is different. Ponchielli was contemporary with middle and later Verdi, but he does not emulate Verdi's earlier style. Also Ponchielli does not usually rise to Verdi's exalted heights musically, but he is still an important composer to consider. Though *La Gioconda* does not appear all that frequently, it is still an opera many people love (and not just because of the "Dance of the Hours" ballet). He requires Verdian-style singing, and in this he is more in league with the older master than the newer style of Mascagni (his pupil) and Puccini. Some people actually denigrate *La Gioconda*, but, given a well-cast performance, one well rehearsed both vocally and dramatically, it is a great show. Coaches must understand the differences in the composers, never assuming the younger composer is the same style as the older, because the differences are just major enough to be quite important.

Verdi, unlike Ponchielli, is very much a mainstay of the repertoire, and as long as the requisite voices can be found, his operas will be performed ... and coaches must learn how to coach singers in his works.

INTERLUDE SIX

THE VANISHING OF LARGE VOICES

It seems somehow appropriate that this Interlude should come directly after the chapter on Verdi and not long before the chapters on Mussorgsky and the Richards, Wagner and Strauss. For the problem facing many opera houses today is the lack of big voices in large enough numbers to satisfy the needs of the various opera theaters. Coaches cannot solve this problem, but a good coach can help those who have the talent for some of this repertoire to develop it better.

Without being a voice teacher per se, a coach can still listen to singers and tell them when they are singing technically incorrectly. This is sometimes done by stressing matching vowels. It can also be accomplished by working on line. There are far too many singers around who sing with little or no sense of line, with a placement that varies from note to note. This is frequently a sign that the singer is pushing their voice for more volume, and that will lead eventually to less volume. The tone the singer should adopt must be round and beautiful, but it cannot be darkened just because a repertoire might demand it. Flexibility is the key to singing, and a dark and weighty tone does not move well. A singer who can sing "Tu che le vanità" from *Don Carlo* should also be able to sing "Ernani, Ernani involami" from *Ernani*. They are the same *Fach* (the German word for vocal classification). But the *Ernani* aria requires some fioritura, and some otherwise wonderful Elisabettas and Leonoras (in *Forza*) just cannot do that. (A list of *Fachs* and some of the roles that fit into each one will be found in Appendix A.)

The coach therefore must listen for such pushing and guide the singer into finding ways to sing the larger repertoire healthily. Certain roles, like Verdi's *Otello*, will always be heavy. And yet, with intelligence, a singer can rely on brightness of tone and what might be called "ping" to add heft to a lighter voice. This is what carries across an orchestra pit. The full-throated approach espoused by a few singers like Franco Corelli (who sang only excerpts from *Otello*) or Mario del Monaco can be very exciting, but those tenors still had a forward "ping" to their voices. Such great tenors as Luciano Pavarotti or Placido Domingo temper their versions of that approach with carefully modulated dynamics and clean diction and rhythm.

Opera history has far too many singers who were blessed with lyric instruments and who have tried to push that limited palate into a more voluminous voice. It does not work, and a coach should advise lyric singers to be careful.

Three important reasons can be given for the vanishing of the larger voices. The first is the lack of patience and perhaps guidance from knowledgeable mentors. Singers want to sing the bigger roles. They are more challenging dramatically and musically (which makes them more *fun!*). The fees for singing the larger roles are higher as well. Unfortunately no Count Almaviva in *Il Barbiere di Siviglia* will ever be given the salary of a Duke of Mantua in *Rigoletto*. So good or excellent Almavivas push their slender instruments into the deceptively heavier role of the Duke. No Zerlina will ever garner the salary of a Gilda, and the singer will therefore push to gain the heavier or higher repertoire.

Another reason is that orchestras are getting louder. The softest volume is no longer as whispered as it once was, and the loudest volume is sometimes quite a deal louder than the composers ever expected. European orchestras are also known to tune almost a half tone sharp, the brilliance being considered laudable. But a singer does not have a peg that can turn their range higher. That, coupled with the louder volume, means that singers are straining for higher notes and more volume, too. The physical nature of a voice just cannot do that. European orchestras are not alone in this perversity, as some American orchestras have done the same.

The third reason for vanishing voices of size rests in the theaters themselves, which have grown for economic reasons, too. In order to pay the salaries that singers and orchestras demand, the houses have grown to well over 3,000 seating capacity. The Metropolitan Opera seats 4,000! It does not take an acoustician to know that a voice that sounded rich, full, large, and round in a 1,500-seat auditorium will sound rather puny in a 4,000-seat auditorium … unless they push! It does not matter how wonderful the acoustics are; the size speaks against it.

Singing styles have changed, and coaches would benefit greatly by listening to some of the older recordings to hear in what fashion people used to sing. A short listen to Mattia Battistini shows that his voice was a much lighter baritone voice than we usually hear today. And yet he sang Don Giovanni, Renato (in *Un Ballo in Maschera*), and the like.

It can be deceptive in listening to recordings to decide just how large a voice really was. Some voices were most assuredly large (Tito Ruffo and Jerome Hines must have had veritable cannons for voices!), but even smaller voices can teach an astute ear what used to be acceptable. It may be that, if we expect to hear some of the operas requiring large voices, we will have to change our ideas again as to what is good or not, incorporating projection and colors more in keeping with the recorded evidence of what composers expected to hear.

A fourth reason for vanishing large voices is much less simple to rectify. The current training in the school systems does little to teach teenagers music or vocal production. This is true in all countries, not just the United States. When music is taught or appreciated by young musicians, it is more frequently the "cool" music of rock, rap, hip-hop, jazz, and even Broadway musicals. While these are also valid musical areas of performance, they do not help train the perceptions needed for performing music called "classical." Vocalists are not sought out even by perceptive high school teachers. If a decent voice exists, it is usually such a diamond in the rough that few teachers identify it as such. And it takes much less musical acumen or training to learn and to perform the modern pop music than it does classical music (particularly opera). Opera is just not part of the active culture to which young people relate. This means a diminishing pool of singers. I have heard excellent voices in people who have simply never had vocal training. The lost potential is almost tragic. At the very least, it explains the limited number of great voices rising to the top today.

9

FRENCH OPERA

FRENCH OPERA REPERTOIRE STEMS FROM a handful of composers. They share certain compositional traits and stylistic considerations while at the same time retaining different specific points about each composer. Berlioz, Meyerbeer, Gounod, Massenet, Bizet, Saint-Säens, Offenbach, Poulenc, Charpentier, and Debussy all share certain ways of writing for voices and even notational peculiarities. Of that group, only Debussy and Poulenc are stylistically different enough to treat in a separate way.

1. NOTATION

The first area that must be covered in a discussion of French opera concerns the tied notes. In Verdi a quarter note tied to an eighth note would equal a dotted quarter note. But in the French style of writing, a quarter tied to an eighth equals a full quarter. Without the tie, the quarter is actually somewhat shorter (roughly a dotted eighth). This is not peculiar to one of these esteemed composers but seems to hold true for them all. (See Figure 14.)

Another important consideration in French opera concerns those syllables that in spoken French are left unsounded, but that in opera are given pitch and limited duration. This occurs so frequently that no example need be given. The reason for this anomaly goes back to stage

Figure 14 French notation — how it is sounded in comparison with what is written and how German and Italian notation would sound.

French. The vanishing syllables were supposed to be sounded so they would project. This is the case, too, in sung theater. For non-native singers, the tendency is to accent those syllables by giving the notes their entire duration. Bearing in mind the above stylistic notation, the notes assigned to those unaccented syllables should in fact be quite short. Though notated frequently as an eighth note, the singer would do better to remember the "vanishing" nature of the syllable and make it a sixteenth.

2. RANGES AND TESSITURAS

An important peculiarity in French music stems from the way those composers wrote for the tenor voice. Those in the above list of composers (and Donizetti and Rossini in their French operas) wrote for the tenors in a tessitura that frequently sits quite high, sometimes as much as a third higher than their Italian or German counterparts. This is due in part to a headier vocal production, and it is also due to a slenderer tonal ideal. The French operatic literature is almost always lyrically attuned. That means that the dramatic thrust found in Verdi (for example) is kept in check in French opera, with none of those heroic and dramatic outbursts such as can be found in *Otello, Pagliacci,* or *Aïda.* One has only to look at the tenor arias from Donizetti's *La Fille du Régiment* or Adam's *Le Postillon de Longjumeau* to realize just how high the "norm" could be. Even Verdi, when he was writing *Don Carlos* and *Les Vêpres Sicilienne,* gave the tenor roles a higher tessitura than was his already higher norm. Auber, in his *Le Philtre* (from which the libretto of Donizetti's *L'Elisir d'amore* is fashioned), also gives Guillaume (Nemorino) an awfully high tessitura, sometimes as much as a third higher than his Italian counterpart.

Oddly, except for the extremely high tenor writing, other roles are frequently given a slightly lower center of vocal gravity. Marguerite in *Faust* may be sung by light lyrics and coloraturas, but the tessitura of the role (as with Massenet's Manon or Debussy's Mélisande) lies much more in the middle voice. Pushing this area of a voice, trying to make it either louder or bigger, will cause it to take on a curdled sound that is not pleasing. The middle voice must be produced securely, with a focused but not a forced sound. The "ping" in the voice carries it across, not the vocal weight. Properly restrained singing will make the brilliant high portions more effective.

It does not take much study of Gounod's operas — notably *Roméo et Juliette* or *Faust* — or those of Massenet — *Manon, Werther,* and *Don Quichotte* — to find highly dramatic moments expressed with a lyric impulse. Bizet's *Pêcheurs des Perles*, despite its somewhat more melodramatic plot, even manages to retain a lyric stance. His *Carmen*, though frequently bellowed as if it were an Italian opera, is just as lyric and benefits from singers treating it in that fashion. There is something about French opera that makes the melodic lines more linear. Juliette's Valse, for example, benefits greatly in lift and forward motion if Juliette considers this linear quality and sings the "Je veux" as two upbeats to the downbeat of "vivre." The rests feel almost scanned to create this lift — almost but not entirely! That linear nature holds true for *Carmen's* arias, Berlioz mélodies, and mélodies from many other French composers. It seems more pronounced than in, shall we say, Verdi.

In this context an explanation of "lyric" is probably in order. By singing lyrically, I mean that the singer pays much attention to words and colors, and that the general dramatic thrust comes through this coloration of text, not from *tutta forza* type of singing appropriate (perhaps) in the overt outbursts of Verdi or the outbursts of Wagner's heroes and gods. In this way the voice can retain a pure and undistorted line, the linear being considered more than single note accents. When done well, the singer is said to be performing with "taste" and the public does not react as wildly as they do for the more extrovert dramatic displays, but the knowing audience member will know just how difficult the "lyric" stance is to maintain.

The French language calls for a certain forward placement for proper sound. Tonally, this puts the voice into a good place, too. The language is more focused than some of the other European languages, and this helps the singer. Many vowels, notably the "a," are brighter than their Italian counterparts. For non-Francophone singers (those who do not speak the language with great fluidity) the difficulty comes in part through the many nasals. A singer cannot sing beautifully and use true nasals. (This holds true even in American country singers!) This point is controversial, because some teachers will insist that a singer *must* use true nasals. But such a sound has limited carrying power and is frequently unattractive. A good coach must have ideas on how to approximate the correct sound without allowing the tone actually to go through the nose. This is accomplished best by singing or saying the nasal correctly and then finding a way to open the vowel some and retain the essence of the true nasal. (This is impossible to demonstrate in print.)

3. REPERTOIRE

Although there are many, the operas that comprise the French repertoire can be summed up in a list of about six operas. Without denigrating Berlioz as a composer, it is a fact that his *Les Troyens, Béatrice et Bénédict*, and so on are not standard repertoire operas. They also have a style all their own, because Berlioz writes in long lines and arching phrases that are patently *his* style. A careful study of his works alone would take several pages and be useful only once in a while.

Similarly, the "other" operas of Gounod, Bizet, and Massenet won't be covered here. The only important French operas to make up the French repertoire are Gounod's *Faust* and *Roméo et Juliette*, Bizet's *Carmen* (but not his *Pêcheurs des Perles* or *Jolie Fille de Perth*), Massenet's *Manon* and *Werther* (but not his *Don Quichotte*), and Offenbach's magnum opus *Les Contes d'Hoffmann* (but not his operettas). These six operas are the core of what we call the French repertoire. The composers Meyerbeer, Delibes, and Halévy may be quite important historically, but in this context there is not enough space to cover even so important an opera as *Les Huguenots*. It just will not come up very frequently. Arias from these operas may appear, but applying knowledge of other French repertoire and some knowledge of bel canto will get the coach through some of these works well. The number of isolated arias by these composers is small and can be easily learned.

All of these operas call forth an acting style that stems from the words themselves. Henry Higgins's famous quote from the Lerner and Loewe musical *My Fair Lady* frequently comes to mind when working in French opera: "The French don't care what they do, actually, as long as they pronounce it properly!"[1]

In this context, to "pronounce it properly" means giving the words their due. The librettos of Eugene Scribe are poetically rather well made, but the plots sometimes reek of the odd letters and mistaken identities. Despite a strong desire to underenunciate the text so no one will know how inane it might seem, a singer has really to work to get these operas across.

In the above list, Jules Barbier and Michel Carré appear three times. They also wrote quite a few other important opera librettos (or *livrets*) for French operas. Their poetry is frequently more inspired than that of Scribe, and their dramatic slant is more modern, hence more acceptable. They really seemed to know how to catch the essence of any dramatic situation. Coaches must always be listening to be certain that texts actually come through. The generally, slightly lower tessitura (except for the tenors and some baritones) was given by the composers in the hope that the singers might have some success at word projection. The dependency on clarity of text is one of the French trademarks.

The formality of French operatic music stems from the early insistence on ballet. Therefore it becomes natural for Manon to sing a gavotte. And various portions of music use the kind of rhythmic verve found in French ballet music. Of course, there are those lengthy ballets in the repertoire of the grand operas. They are always a problem to stage, and yet they are so integral to some of the plots or musical balance that leaving them out can mean a severe hole in the music.

Another important trademark of all French music can best be explained with this maxim: If the composer does not ask for rubato or ritardandos, do not include them. The stretching of a phrase is quite acceptable in Italian literature, but, though it is a major temptation, particularly in some songs of Fauré, it is not acceptable in French operas or solo instrumental works. Some works may seem to call for a highly rhapsodic style, but the greatest teachers of French music argue otherwise. The composers usually are so specific about portamento, ritardando, tenuto, and the like, that they do not need a "helping hand" from a performer. This means that an astute coach must be firm against such added improvements, but must also be certain that all markings are followed. A score like *Manon* by Massenet is so replete with markings that it becomes a real accomplishment to reproduce even half of them. Totality is the goal.

Tradition is not a license to avoid the rubato rule. In *Roméo et Juliette*, Juliette's Valse has a traditional ritardando every time she ascends to the high A. Yet a listen to those sopranos who actually studied the aria with Gounod shows that they do not take this liberty. Sopranos and directors may want it, and conductors may allow it, but, facing that dilemma, my suggestion is that moderation is better than the huge ritardando. I prefer no change of tempo because I find that the youthful energy is served better with no "romantic" interpolation.

This penchant for purity of line and expression and its absence in singers (even those of the nineteenth century) is at least in part the explanation for Rossini's strange forty-year silence. Living in Paris at the time of his last success (*Guillaume Tell*, 1829), he despaired of singers taking the time to learn a proper technique to continue the really refined singing to which he had become accustomed. The newer demand for volume, *squillando*, and so on all led away from the well-modulated and poised tone. Meyerbeer also felt this movement, and his later operas reflect a less demanding attitude toward singers. Berlioz, composing early enough to avoid such trends, actually can be considered one of the best examples of this refined style of singing. His vocal writing shows up faulty techniques mercilessly, and that can be a major reason that his operas are not more frequently performed.

Bizet's *Carmen* is so frequently performed that many comments are not in order. But the slenderer vocal production alluded to in this chapter actually helps project the music to a degree that the overt sobbing, shouting, and chesty singing employed in some performances can never do. The opera is popular, but woe betide the singer or coach who thinks it is easy. Carmen is not just a vamp, but is a complex character. She may be a mezzo-soprano role, but the tessitura is not so uncomfortable even for some sopranos. Tenors tackling Don José should realize that trying to overpower the role will lead to real problems. The problem with the role is that it starts out as a lyric tenor role and ends as a dramatic. The toreador, Escamillo, is a low baritone role, one too frequently shouted through instead of sung.

For *Pélleas et Mélisande* Debussy took his compositional cue in part from Wagner's *Parsifal* and in part from Mussorgsky's *Boris Godunov*. The former has a constant orchestral underpinning (one cannot call it accompaniment) that enlightens and highlights every thing that is sung. The vocal line rides over this carpet with quite natural inflection. The voices are kept in the central voice for the most part, enabling the singer to project the text carefully and completely. The naturalistic way of writing rhythms for the voices stems from Debussy's study of Wagner's *Parsifal* and Mussorgsky's work. Debussy may not provide quite as many shifts of tempo as Mussorgsky, but he certainly takes his cue on how to write constantly shifting subtle moods from the Russian master. The sometimes broken lines and short, angular nature of some sung phrases stem directly from the late Wagner style (see the excerpt in the chapter on Wagner). If the orchestral palate derives from the Impressionistic school, the vocal writing comes from the two masters mentioned. A coach must never underestimate the difficulty of this kind of writing. Particularly in the later acts, the propulsive nature of the music combined with the emotionally rising drama can make singers forget to learn the count of the music securely. Without absolutely secure rhythm the music becomes a terrible guessing game, and music of this nature cannot hold together that way.

The French language has no real or natural accent. It seems to be a less inflected language than, say, English or German. Despite the truth of this statement, certain words do require some correct accent, even if the composer writes against the normal accent. (See earlier comments about Bizet and *Carmen*.) Coaches must understand the correct accents and help singers achieve them. This attitude toward the French language explains also the dramatic reserve sometimes found in the operas. It also means that, in roles like Mephistopheles, the singer must act up the projection of text, but he must not (as the first singer of Mephisto apparently did) overact himself. It is a fine line, and the difference in that stylistic concern may explain why French opera is not always as popular as Italian. Overt outbursts work well in Italian operas but not in French ones.

I must mention two operas here because they are revived occasionally and because, although they share certain traits with the other French composers, they also have difficulties all their own. Gustave Charpentier is noted for only his opera *Louise*. The writing of the opera is a combination of traditional French, verismo, and even a little minimalism (years before such a style came into being). An aria like "Depuis le jour" sounds easy until a soprano tries to project the pure line of the piece. Then the true difficulty comes to the fore. A coach must not underestimate such a section of music as the opening of act 2. It will require many hours of coaching. The music is quite difficult, the accompaniment does not help the singers at all, and the sung language is not "stage French" but "street French," with requisite contractions such as we hear in American all the time. Francophone singers may have little trouble with the language, but the gossip session is formidable.

Poulenc's opera *Dialogues des Carmélites* is yet another case. The music is frequently gently lyric, but it rises to very intense emotional heights. The orchestra frequently carries the melodic thread (as in Puccini), with the voices picking up portions of the melodies. Just as frequently, however, the voices may rattle off various highly parlando phrases and then jump back to the melody. The opera is mostly through-composed, and there are very few arias. The characters, however, are vividly drawn, and a singer must try to achieve the various levels of dramatic conviction each role requires. As an example, Madame Lidoine's aria "Mes filles" from act 3 is a perfect depiction of her strength and courage, her implacable and unflappable nature rising to the horror facing her and the other nuns. (Leontyne Price, who performed the role early in her career, recorded this aria, bridging into the second section to complete it, eliminating the jailer.) A coach should take the metronome numbers as fact. Ricordi originally published the piano score without over half of the orchestral interludes. They have recently been added, and, acquiring a score, a singer or coach should look for the most recent "ristampa" date. The newer version still retains a few major mistakes, and the coach may want to study the orchestral score to find these.

(Production teams and coaches take note: The sound of the guillotine in the final, terrifying scene is accomplished by sliding a machete down a metal rod of roughly 36-inch length, landing in a block of wood at the bottom. A microphone placed quite close should pick up the sound, amplification making it the desired loudness.)

10

MUSSORGSKY AND THE RUSSIANS

THE FIRST IMPORTANT HURDLE IN Russian opera will always be the language itself. Cyrillic is a different alphabet, and that alone makes Russian difficult. Add to that vowel sounds that are totally different from Western languages, and we begin to gather an appreciation of the problems facing Western musicians when confronting Russian opera.

In reality, most opera houses will deal with only a few Russian operas. Until recently, even the Metropolitan Opera would perform these works in English. But around thirty years ago that changed. The most commonly performed operas in the Russian language are *Boris Godunov* and *Khovanschina* by Mussorgsky, and *Yevghenyi (Eugene) Onegin* and *Pique Dame (Pikovaya Dama)* by Tchaikovsky. The operas of Rimsky-Korsakov and Rachmaninoff (and a few others) are so seldom performed outside of Russia itself that they do not bare close scrutiny here. The other operas of Tchaikovsky are seldom dusted off even there. Prokofiev's operas, notably *Love for Three Oranges, War and Peace,* and *Betrothal in a Monastery*, or Stravinsky's *Mavra,* are frequently performed, if at all, in translation, though that is changing. Glinka is historically quite important, but he does not figure prominently into anyone's repertoire.

The first thing a coach must understand about Russian opera is the give and take of the dialogue. Therefore, even if dealing with the operas in English, the coach must make the singer realize that one phrase may answer the previous one in a slightly slower or faster tempo. The switch from one character to another *may* not continue at a metronomic pace either. There may even be a slight pause between measures. One measure may push ahead in a rather sprightly tempo and the next may languish. An easy example to study (not produced here due to the length of the exchange) can be found in act 1, scene 1 of *Onegin*. In the conversations leading into Olga's aria and after it, Tatiana is filled with ennui and Olga is chiding in a good-natured way, while Larina and Filipyevna are expressing differing degrees of concern about Tatiana's emotional languor. The tempo throughout the exchange must ebb and flow depending on the nature of the words. Even within a statement, there may be need for a brief dramatic breath. Each character must think of what she will say before spouting it.

Upon the approach of Lensky, there is a switch to $^6/_8$. Here the rhythm becomes much more precise and difficult. Tchaikovsky expects the anxiety of approaching "company" to infect all of them with a kind of terror. In an almost comic fashion, he has the music plunge ahead to a dramatic stop, effectively placing the women in a receiving line. (The effect also seems to give them a pasted-on smile that radiates the kind of "hello" that is supposed to mask comically their earlier confusion.) Tchaikovsky just never embraces the Russian culture the way the Russian Five did — Cui, Balakirev, Borodin, Rimsky-Korsakov, and Mussorgsky.

Modeste Mussorgsky's *Boris Godunov* is considered a seminal work at least in part because of the completely original way Mussorgsky dealt with the text. He is perfectly able to keep a steady tempo for extended passages. The Polonaise and Love Duet in the Polish Act, Varlaam's song about Kazan, and Fyodor's clapping song are examples of such moments. But the great monologues of Boris himself require total immersion in the text.

Listening to the great monologue as an example for study, with score in hand, will show any coach what I mean. The music ebbs and flows, depending on whether Boris is elated or depressed, indignant or forthright. Boris addresses Fyodor in one fashion, and muses on the nature of his regime in another.

The lengthy aria may show at least to some extent how important the words are. Mussorgsky, unlike Massenet, Verdi, or Puccini, wrote only some of what he expected to be performed dramatically. Part of this stems from his being only a part-time composer. But he also may have thought that what he wanted was so obvious, depending on the phrasing of the words, that he "knew" the singer would inflect the words properly. He also knew that a knowledgeable singer would separate words that needed to be separated. It is for this reason that coaches who do not know Russian need to find Russian speakers to help in the coaching of this literature.

It bears mention here that the Cyrillic alphabet is not *so* difficult to master, and idiomatic translations can help a coach learn much about the language itself. This is not to say that a Russian expert is not necessary, just that initial work really can be done without recourse to such tutors. A coach should learn to make a good transliteration (Russian words written in the Latin alphabet) from which to start.

The aforementioned example also shows that tempi can fluctuate considerably, even in places where the composer does not so indicate. In the German Romantic tradition this kind of rubato is usually based on the melodic and harmonic contours of the music itself, but in Russian music, as with the later French style with which it has some close affinity, the rubato is all based solely on verbal nuance. This rubato can even be found in music without text if that music is meant to reflect a verbal source — Orthodox chant.

The Russian Five and Tchaikovsky were always at odds, and in comparing Mussorgsky and Tchaikovsky one can understand how that is. Mussorgsky leans heavily on the folk forms. Except in a piece like the monologue from Boris, he relies heavily on Russian dance, Orthodox melodies, and folk song styles. These are simple in structure, and they can be readily assimilated by an audience. One has only to think of the Innkeeper's song, Varlaam's Kazan Song, the Clapping Song, Feodor's Popinka narrative, Marina's aria, or the Polonaise to understand this. *Khovanschina* has these kinds of pieces in it as well. The folk element is always lurking near the surface, throwing into relief quite sharply the dialogue-type passages.

Tchaikovsky uses folk melodies some, too. But whole scenes can happen without one reference to such melodies. The harmonic palette, while clearly "Russian," is also influenced by Western practices. The Quartet, Letter Scene, or the final duet from *Onegin* are all composed in a strictly Russian Romantic style, lingering on certain words and phrases and relying on the considerable verbal projection of the singer. They do not, however, have folk or church elements present. Tchaikovsky reserved those for the few times he needed to indicate certain social situations or milieus. In *Onegin,* the chorus of peasants in act 1 follows the folk-inspired element closely. And in the famous *Romeo and Juliet Overture*, he alludes to the Orthodox chant.

Beyond the folk elements, one will find strong characters in Russian opera, living their lives and plotting their schemes with great power. Tchaikovsky's Hermann (*Pique Dame*) or Onegin are great character studies. His Joan of Arc (*Orleanskaya Dieva* — *Maid of Orleans*) is an equally strong role, with wonderful opportunities both for singing and for dramatic characterization. Mussorgsky's Boris is of course strong, the dramatic possibilities being as deep as in a role like Hamlet. But of equal interest are other roles, like Shuisky, Marina, Dmitri, Shaklovity, Khovansky senior, and Marfa. A coach must understand the dramatic possibilities of each, the vocal demands of each, and the style of each composer, and help the singer to come to grips with these great operas.

It will help a coach immensely if he can find ways to transliterate the Russian into the Roman alphabet. This will help initial pronunciation. Follow this with a good translation (literal and idiomatic) in order to understand the complexities of the scenes.

The coach will initially find that coaching Russian opera is quite difficult, but, once acquaintance with the style and language becomes more ingrained, the coach will begin to understand the reasons for the "traditional" elements that appear in so many places. It is partially for this reason that the best editions possible should be sought out. This will ensure that what the composers actually put down on paper will come through and be translated into real drama.

11

RICHARD WAGNER AND RICHARD STRAUSS

In dealing with the late German Romantic school of Wagner, Strauss, and also Humperdinck, we must first acknowledge that the coach must do some considerable "woodshedding" in order to play those composers' scores. Learning to play these scores is a task comparable to learning several of Beethoven's late sonatas all at once. It is true that in playing a score at the piano, a coach does not have to play every note written. The reduction is supposed to show what the singer will hear and frequently goes beyond the capabilities of even the best coaches to play every note. Still, achieving even a modest degree of expertise at playing the scores will require hours of practice. It takes time and effort to get all of the chords correctly played and to find just what is important to play. This is sometimes referred to as playing the *melos*, the sounding composition, as opposed to every note the composer wrote. Pride may make a coach want to play everything, but it is probably not going to be possible.

Part of the reason these scores are so difficult is the increased chromaticism found in the operas of these composers. Printed scores are not always perfect either at getting all of the notes printed correctly. Sometimes a little rearrangement of the exact writing can make little aural difference but can make an immense difference in the difficulty of what is played.

Another reason for the difficulty in playing comes from the contrapuntal method these composers used for composing, an orchestral fabric that includes combined musical motives and layered textures. A notable example of this is found in the opening of act 3 of *Der Rosenkavalier* (an audition piece for coaches!), and includes some extremely difficult passage work, followed by 4/4 time in the main orchestra and a waltz from the orchestra backstage. Without playing necessarily all of both, a coach must suggest that both are continuing and existing simultaneously, fighting for supremacy. The orchestral writing becomes not so much a true accompaniment (as in bel canto operas or Verdi) but a running tapestry, commenting on the action and emotions of the characters. This accompaniment sometimes becomes quite dense and heavily orchestrated. It also may take over for whole sections, transitions from one scene to another or lengthy passages of stage action (and occasionally inaction) that takes time to unwind. The aforementioned *Rosenkavalier* excerpt, though no words are sung during its playing, has to be learned because it will be played at staging rehearsals and must be clear for the people to learn the staging of the pantomime that takes place.

With an orchestral underpinning of this nature, the vocal lines are no longer just melodic utterances. They become a counterpoint in themselves to the orchestral fabric. The voice must ride a line that floats on top of the orchestra one moment and then may plunge into the middle of that texture the next. Such vocal lines bear little relationship to songs or regular arias. And the parlando nature of many of these lines makes the rhythm quite difficult. A look at the role of Baron Ochs in *Der Rosenkavalier* will show how challenging his role is for these exact reasons. Not only is he rhythmically difficult from beginning to end, spouting first instructions to a lawyer, then lecherous, leering jibes at Sophie and then, later still, his pompous feelings of injustices against himself, but he must also sing most of his music in Viennese dialect (quite far from high German). All of this must flow from his mouth in an easy stream (filled with many written epithets) and in a wide-ranging vocal display that includes an exposed low D. Parlando in the Richards must not degenerate into the kind of singing that seems as much barking as singing. Both of the excerpts found later in this chapter, one from *Parsifal* and one from *Salome*, invite the kind of approximate pitch singing appropriate in Berg, but it is not appropriate in Wagner or Strauss, where accurate pitches, rhythms, and good singing must always be remembered.

The poetry is important, too, and can be a stumbling block for the singer learning the music. Wagner was his own librettist, of course, and he strove for some very deep moments of introspection. Monologues like those found in Hans Sachs (*Die Meistersinger von Nürnberg*) or Wotan (the *Ring*) bring out the soul of the character, inner turmoil always being at the forefront. When his characters become heated in high emotion (particularly sensual), however, they can lapse into what, to a translator, seems like babble. Passages of the love duet from *Tristan und Isolde* are nearly nonsensical divorced from the dramatic situation. Earlier texts, while simpler in some ways, are no less difficult to make real than the later ones. He may have learned to become a better composer, but his poetry still carries with it moments of awkwardness even into *Parsifal*.

This is not to say that everything a singer must learn is related to pitches and poetry. Wagner has given some characters "musical instruments" to play. Siegfried must play the anvil and Hans Sachs must play on the bottom of a shoe, both playing with hammers of differing nature. Wagner writes the rhythm, however, and, though recordings can cover this well with a percussionist, in live performances it is the singer who must "schlag" in rhythm. It is sometimes quite difficult, and the coach must be certain that the singer can "beat" their role as well as sing it. In *Meistersinger*, the singer performing Sextus Beckmesser must also convincingly act as if he is playing a lute, all the while following the conductor. (Beckmesser's Serenade is a major difficulty for any conductor due to the stop-and-start nature of the excerpt, and then because it leads into a fugal riot of monumental difficulty.)

Strauss was frequently working on texts of Hugo von Hofmannsthal, and those librettos are quite different from Wagner. *Salome* (text by Oscar Wilde as translated by Hedwig Lachmann) already sets the tone for Richard Strauss's operas by combining considerable emphasis on central women's roles, and by relying on orchestral underpinning. But from *Elektra* onward, the story unfolds with greater emotional depth, and the text is frequently replete with layers of meaning or thought. It also has moments that elicited from Strauss what one friend of mine called "noise music," that curious orchestral writing with no themes, just sound painting. Whips crack in *Elektra*, birds fly around (at least in Herod's mind) in *Salome*, and Leopold and other servants of Baron Ochs chase the girls in *Der Rosenkavalier*. They are not great moments of drama, and Strauss seems to have written through them with little musical care — they are just mini–tone poems. Still the coach may have to make sense of them for the singer. The layers involved in understanding a character like the Marschallin (in *Rosenkavalier*) or an entire opera like *Die Frau ohne Schatten* can take quite a while to unravel.

Projection of voice through these dense textures must come from a clear enunciation of the text. This means both consonant/vowel diction and the more important "thought diction" mentioned elsewhere in this volume. With texts constructed in the fashion of Wagner or Hofmannsthal, attention must be given to the lively words, those that can elicit a vocal coloring of the text. The coach should realize that Wagner and Strauss, no matter what their reputation for heavy orchestral writing may be, actually allow the singer to come through with only a modest amount of heft. Birgit Nilsson (well versed in both composers) even commented once that Elektra, after a few initial outbursts, becomes a relatively lyric role and should be sung that way. While this observation may not allow lyric voices to sing the heavier repertoire, it does mean that larger voices do not have to give 100 percent throughout an entire evening. It also means that, if a smaller voice attempts to sing the large roles (Siegfried, Brünnhilde, Elektra, Salome, Tannhäuser, Wotan, Hagen, etc.), it will suffer vocal collapse. Coaches must understand this and guide the potential Wagner and Strauss singer into the correct repertoire choices, helping them also to learn methods to get through such stiff assignments.

Though the general vocal writing would be difficult in any case, both composers require a very large orchestra. Whereas Verdi's early works require perhaps fifty players (and some houses might use fewer), his later operas *require* only a few more than that (say, sixty-five). Bel canto composers used probably a maximum of forty-five players. But Wagner used orchestras of around seventy-five for even his early works, and the later ones, particularly the *Ring* cycle, require around ninety players. Strauss, particularly in *Elektra* and *Salome*, requires around 100 players. Imagine trying to sing over an orchestra that size! The purpose of this size is for a wide range of color, not necessarily volume. But still it means a bigger pit and the potential for very dense textures. The length of a work like *Die Frau ohne Schatten* makes learning and playing such an opera difficult for any orchestra or for any coach trying to play a reduction. (Orchestral players at the Metropolitan Opera have described playing the three acts of Strauss's *Die Frau ohne Schatten* as an exercise comparable to playing three Mahler symphonies back to back.)

Wagner had a solution to the problem of size/volume himself. He designed a stage and pit for his Bayreuth Festspielhaus that had a unique construction. The stage, unlike most theaters, is not above the level of the audience, but it is actually at a level that continues down from the slant of the auditorium floor. This idea came to him from the Greek amphitheaters, whose playing areas are also at the bottom of the audience slant. This allows the sound to radiate up from the singers as in that Greek amphitheater. The orchestra pit, though in front of the stage, is lower yet, with only a slight, curved cover sticking up enough for a singer to see the conductor. This has the advantages of diminishing the amount of sound pouring from the orchestra, of blending that sound more completely, and of making the orchestra invisible to the audience. Since the pit opening is so much smaller, the viewer is unaware that a pit exists, and thus they become unaware just how tall a *giant* is or how short a *dwarf* might be. This also makes the action on stage closer to the audience. Considering the importance of the words in Wagnerian monologues, this is an added bonus, since the audience can see the emotions registering on the face of the singers much more clearly. In addition, the sight lines are unbroken by pillars or other obstructions. The depth of the stage can be opened to the depth of three stages. Thus, when Lohengrin is "seen in the distance," he is actually visible at quite a real distance.

The Bayreuth pit is also constructed with a peculiar shape all its own. Instead of the entire orchestra being on one level playing area, the orchestra pit is tiered down in three or four tiers, the brass and percussion taking the lowest area and strings the highest. This aids in the balancing problems within the orchestral fabric and between the pit and the voices. The sound also shoots first up onto the stage and then goes out into the auditorium proper. This means that the orchestral size and volume are taken care of by Wagner in a way no other theater can manage. The oddity is that no other theater has even attempted this solution, particularly the idea of the stage being lower than the audience. (The fact that the seats are uncomfortable seems to be a malicious idea from Wagner to keep the audience awake during the extensive monologues and dialogues.) Yet it would seem to be a viable idea for any number of theaters, not just the hallowed halls on the "Green Hill" in Bayreuth. (The covered pit has yet another blessing: Its structure means the orchestral players can dress rather casually — in the summer! — and still not be seen.)

The vocal production demanded of these scores is something a coach must consider. In recent years the older school of nonsinging in Wagner operas has vanished. People have begun to remember that Wagner grew up at the end of the bel canto era. That is to the good. Wagner particularly requires a large, healthy voice, produced with some ease and with good line, verbal projection, and with enough voice to carry over the orchestra pit to the back of the house. Some roles (notably Tannhäuser and Siegfried) are simply voice killers. And yet they are not impossible, if a singer takes time and learns not only the music of the roles but also how to sing them properly.

Coaches must understand what kind of vocal size these operas demand, and find ways for the potentially gifted interpreters of them to sing them. Some recent singers, such as Deborah Voigt and Ben Heppner, have proved that not only is singing Wagner possible, but he can be sung beautifully and passionately without totally destroying their voices. The key, I think, is to understand when to give voice and when to relax, allowing diction to carry the voice across the pit.

In Wagner's earliest operas, *Die Feen, Das Liebesverbot,* and *Rienzi,* the recitatives were quite wooden and uninteresting. Some of this can still be found even in *Der Fliegende Holländer, Tannhaüser,* and *Lohengrin.* But after those operas, starting with the *Ring,* Wagner worked the recitative more completely into the whole fabric. These passages take some work to make the singer sound more natural.

In the following excerpt from *Parsifal* (Figure 15), I have included two accompaniments. The various ways the original rhythms are simplified in the lower version can guide the coach in how to make his job easier and perhaps also make the singer hear more clearly the tonality of the accompaniment.

This excerpt was chosen because it invites the "barking" style of Wagner singing. It is also so chromatic that singing pitches are difficult to find. In the second measure, the basic chord is an A_7 chord, despite the initial D#. Parsifal can find his pitch here relatively easily. But he must sing that first "Ja!" with an onset (a flexing of the diaphragm to start the air and tone). He may color that word in some way, but it must have tonal substance and not be mostly hot air.

In measure three, the persistent E on top makes finding the D in the voice difficult unless the singer considers the left hand to be a G minor chord (first inversion) without an added sixth. The vocal line in measure three must be quite sustained, the rest barely registering. The violins in measure four actually help the singer to be certain he is on the right pitch. Halfway through the bar the chordal structure outlines an $E\flat_9$ chord, the voice taking the fifth.

Measure five begins in the voice merely a step up from the previous measure. Luckily the voice fits in with the orchestral tonality. "Deutlich erkenn' ich ihn, …" is a short phrase, as is the following one, but they must be fully supported, though not loud, and they must further the thought from one phrase to the next. In measure seven, the voice must not pound into the F#, as the text does not warrant it. The pitches through these measures are not too difficult to find. "… die Lippe" is frequently approximate in pitch, but the accompaniment is quite clear and should help the singer.

Figure 15 Wagner — excerpt from *Parsifal* (Act Two).

Measures nine through twelve are much more problematic for the singer. The singer, possibly already tired from earlier in the act, tends to deliver these notes in a parlando fashion wholly inappropriate to the intense moment. Therefore they push the parlando, thinking this will get through. A steady, singing tone, centered on every pitch and rhythm will make the singer's voice sound forth quite nicely. Particularly nasty is the scalar passage on "… flatterten lachend die Locken." It changes "tonality" halfway up, and singers don't always center their voices

Figure 15 (continued). Wagner — excerpt from *Parsifal* (Act Two).

squarely on the pitches. The line can actually be sung in a sustained and lyric fashion, culminating in the top G#, but it will require several passes to get the pitches correct.

Measures twelve through fourteen are less wicked rhythmically, although the nonchord notes are still quite prominent. Measure fourteen is usually sung with the syncopated notes being leaned on and the

Figure 15 (continued). Wagner — excerpt from *Parsifal* (Act Two).

smaller notes being less. This makes sense with the textual accents and gives the singer a semblance of sobbing.

Throughout, the singer must be singing with a free tone and still convey the impression that he is convulsed in agony. For this reason the singer must initially learn the role carefully, with all rhythms, pitches, and words sung with little emotion. Once the technique is up

Figure 15 (continued). Wagner — excerpt from *Parsifal* (Act Two).

to the challenge of a passage, the singer can then turn on the dramatic "engines" and find the pathway to the truth of the dramatic moment.

It is also important for a coach to know that Wagner, while generally avoiding the highest notes of a voice's register, may instead put the singer directly in the *passaggio* of the voice and leave them there. Tannhäuser sings whole ensembles in the E to G range and then is asked to rise to A's. This takes its toll on a singer as much or more than the size of the orchestra.

Humperdinck, known almost exclusively for his *Hänsel und Gretel*, requires less than his mentor, Wagner, but his textures are more than reminiscent of his teacher, some almost direct quotes sounding clearly forth. The singers must all be well schooled in their roles, and no one can ever take the score for granted just because it is a "children's opera." It is curious to note that, in the joyous waltz near the end of the opera, I have found that many younger singers do not have waltzing in their bones. They understand it, but their bodies don't quite catch the *Schwung* of the piece. There are also some discrepancies between scores in this section, Peters being generally more correct, but the orchestral *partitura* being more correct than any piano-vocal score.

The operas of Strauss (who was the first conductor of *Hänsel und Gretel*) require less amplitude of sound (mostly), but they sometimes require that voices sing wonderfully long lines. The famous trio from *Der Rosenkavalier* is not only the climactic moment of the opera, but it also has some of the most heavenly intertwining of vocal lines in the operatic literature — and some of the longest, too. How a singer does this kind of singing may stem from a learned coach helping him or her through the learning process. Enduring the long phrases takes calm and careful practice. And it is sometimes up to the singer to flatly say, "I can't make it through the phrase at such a slow tempo." It may seem like being a diva, but it is actually self-preservation, and conductors usually follow the request.

Figure 16 comes from Strauss's opera *Salome*. The first note is actually the last note of the famous "Dance of the Seven Veils." The accompaniment is a maze of cross rhythms, chromatics, and impossible fingerings. The left hand in measure four and following should be brought out, possibly letting some of the triplets go in favor of those bass notes and perhaps the important pitches in the right hand.

Until measure nine in fact the accompaniment does not double one note of the vocal part. How, then, is the singer to find his pitch? At the beginning of the excerpt, the crashing chord is an A minor chord. From that point on, through measure seven of the excerpt, Herod outlines A major tonality, the only note not fitting the actual chord being the F# in measure five. In measure eight, the singer veers away from A major just when the accompaniment accents an A_7 chord. But the next measure actually lets the voice and accompaniment unify in a real tonality, the distant G♭ major (although it is a brief landing point). In a passage like this, the accompaniment being rather as much a hindrance as a help, the singer must at times feel his own shifting

Figure 16 Strauss — excerpt from *Salome*.

tonalities, finding pitches here and there in the orchestra upon which to grab the tonal center as a reality check.

Of course, the opera *Elektra* is much harder than this. But the later operas of Richard Strauss can be deceptively difficult, too. I have coached the Najade, Dryade, and Echo scene (the one announcing the arrival of Bacchus) many times, and I have never had a trio think it was easy at first; some have been almost in tears and some have thought

2

Figure 16 (continued). Strauss — excerpt from *Salome*.

that they "could never learn it." But with careful and slow study, they all gradually find the path through the maze of shifting tonalities and verbal phrases to find their way to enjoying the scene.

The operas of Alban Berg — *Wozzeck* and *Lulu* — are written in a style that is an extension of the Strauss heard in *Elektra* — and musically deal with extreme chromatics, though only *Lulu* is actually written in Schönberg's twelve-tone system. Though there are still some long lines we associate with Richard Strauss, the drama and musical style demand that the vocal lines will be very angular, with wide leaps, difficult tessituras, and difficult pitches to find. The vocal writing also incorporates Berg's usage of that wonderful Schönberg invention: *Sprechstimme*. This is literally "speaking voice" and means that pitches, indicated with an *X* instead of a note head, are to be more spoken but less on pitch than the usual parlando style incorporated into other operas. The tone is frequently produced without much vibrato, and a certain sing-song quality is heard. Unfortunately, this *Sprechstimme* allows for singers to sing *at* pitches rather than *on* pitches and invites very free interpretations of Berg's written ideas. A simple study of existing recordings will point this out. But there is a major reason for this inappropriately wayward attitude to pitches, and that is the singer's immersion in the drama.

Berg was dealing in the new era of Freudian psychology, and that is represented in the moody ramblings of Wozzeck or of Lulu. To a tamer extent (except in *Elektra*) so does Strauss. Wagner used little psychology and a lot of philosophy. This is evident in Hans Sachs or Wotan, but sometimes extends to the very nature of the story lines themselves. The psychodrama elicits from Berg a vocal and orchestral writing that is extremely difficult to master, and yet in these operas singing the notes

correctly and musically is quite far from the eventual goal of projecting these manic and disturbed characters. It is a means to an end but
not the end itself.

It is not really the job of the coach to get into heated discussions
with the singer about the dramatic slant of an opera beyond the nature
of the character itself. Whether a character might be a grotesque stereotype or not may need some discussion, but the director will take his
or her slant on things, and the coach can leave it at that. There are
many people who say, for example, that Mime (notably in *Siegfried*)
and Sextus Beckmesser (in *Die Meistersinger*) are examples of Wagner's anti-Semitic stance. This sort of thing can bear discussion to a
degree (and perhaps *should* be discussed), but creation of the character itself is the important thing, and you cannot play a stereotype. A
singer must portray a real character, and if that character has some
stereotypical attributes, so be it. Wagner's avowed anti-Semitism was
well known from his verbal writings (though that may be as much a
diatribe against Meyerbeer as against all Jews in music), but it does not
mean that every bizarre character is an anti-Semitic slur.

Berg's *Lulu* and Wagner's music dramas have a formal layout that
needs to be understood as well. *Lulu* is dramatically constructed on a
large arch with elements being presented at either end of the arch that
depend on the other end to be present. This is the reason Friedrich
Cerha's completion of the orchestration of Berg's opera was so important. The form needed it.

Wagner's forms can be even more immense. The *Ring* cycle is considered to be in the form of a symphony, which means that fourteen
hours of music are all related. The "bar form" used so frequently by real
Mastersingers is explained in act 3 of *Die Meistersinger* quite clearly,
but some people have actually pointed out that the entire opera *is* one!

It is just as impossible for a singer to play a form as it is for him
or her to portray a stereotype. But a coach must understand to some
degree how each of these things are manifest in the opera and, if necessary, be able to point it out to a singer. It may not be necessary for a
singer to consider *Siegfried* as the scherzo of a symphony, but it may
help in dramatic or even vocal ways.

The sheer size of these Germanic operas makes learning and playing
them quite difficult. Understanding them on at least some level beyond
just notes is also a difficult assignment, and yet it is one a coach must
take on to coach these great works.

12

PUCCINI AND THE VERISMO SCHOOL

THE OPERAS OF GIACOMO PUCCINI were written in the post-Ibsen era, when realistic reactions and interactions were dramatically the norm. Drama had not yet reached the psychodrama stage of Freudian-based works, but it was certainly a far cry from the dramatic style Verdi had chosen as the basis for his operas. The major sources Puccini chose for his operas were Murger, Belasco, and Sardou. As with Verdi (except in Verdi's Shakespeare operas), he chose the newest plays and novels of the era and transformed them into great dramas. Where Verdian characters could take time to wax poetic or take a stance and blatantly trumpet their resolve to the rafters, Puccini's characters are more natural, acting in an almost normal time frame and with little real bombast. They take time for poetic utterances, but they also act in a real way to real dramatic situations. This was the style and era known as verismo.

What exactly is verismo? It actually began at least as far back as 1875. *Carmen*, although French instead of Italian, is sometimes thought of as verismo in style. In a verismo opera characters are, for the most part, ordinary people, with no kings or queens, no dukes or earls. Not one of those can be found anywhere in Puccini until we get to *Turandot*, and that focuses on the lower end of the caste system, preferring to place emphasis on the people behind the figure.

The dramatic situations were also different. Although Verdi and Puccini both supplied us with the major examples of consumptive heroines, most of Verdi's plots are about political intrigues, actions at a court, mad gypsies, and the like. These are hardly the things to which the late-nineteenth-century person on the street could relate. But, then, this also reflects the difference between audiences. The royal theaters of the eras of Mozart, Rossini, and early Verdi had become the public theaters, and this was reflected in subject matter chosen. In some ways, Verdi's *Rigoletto* (1850) might actually be considered the first verismo opera, so the differences are not as great as one might think dramatically. Musically, the drama took total precedence over the musical forms, and that is a major difference between earlier composers and the operas of Puccini and his followers in the verismo school.

Puccini's operas deal with people in personal crises. Whether dealing with the conflict between lovers, politically charged events, or the betrayal of one lover by another, the drama always moves on a personal level. In *Tosca*, for example, the Napoleonic movement provides a time-centered background for the opera, but the actual drama takes place in private areas. Act 1, though frequently played in the main nave of a church, is supposed to take place in a private chapel off the nave. This may be less spectacular to watch, but it focuses the drama into a smaller place and makes Scarpia's singing in the "Te Deum" a fight against the demons within himself rather than a struggle against the vocal forces behind him. Act 2 is in the confined area of Scarpia's apartment, and act 3, although in the open air, is at the top of the building, and the only means of leaving the top parapet are the stairs or leaping over the edge — both of which are used.

This new drama required a new acting style. When Rodolfo sings "Che gelida manina," he may be in a poetic mood (he's a poet after all), but the poetry is never quite as high-flown as his vocal line. Directly before the aria, he had behaved in a fashion both humorous and very typical for a man alone with a young woman in his own apartment. His finding and hiding of the key has an attitude quite new for the times, to say nothing of the extinguishing of his candle even earlier (usually played as no accident but as a willful improvement of the situation on Rodolfo's part). This natural acting style might seem to mean less hysteria and over-the-top acting. But that is not quite true. The high emotions of Tosca, of Giorgetta in *Il Tabarro,* or of Madama Butterfly arise out of intensely driven plots that build to a climax. These climaxes are all rooted in normal reactions to extreme stimuli. Even ecstatic moments like Suor Angelica's final apotheosis arise out of a story line based in interaction between normal people in an abnormal situation, and that situation is not unheard of in Puccini's times. When Cavaradossi lunges at Scarpia in act 2, it is the reaction of a politically savvy man tasting a moment of vindication and triumph. His "Vittoria" may be short-lived, but he reacts within the bounds of a fanatical but real individual.

All of this must be understood by a singer and by a coach. I have begun with the acting style instead of the music because that is the most important difference between Puccini and Verdi. There are other important differences to come, but understanding where the drama comes from is essential in Puccini's operas. The odd mistaken identities and secret letters of Scribe-type librettos (from the mid-nineteenth century) are nowhere in evidence. Indeed, practically the only letter of importance in Puccini appears in act 2 of *Butterfly*, and that is, in part, to prepare Butterfly and the audience for the change of situations that will present itself in the final scene.

Musically, it is important to note that Puccini bases many of his arias on the simpler canzona of his time. The Neapolitan and Sicilian songs are never far from Puccini's musical palette. The lines are almost never in a strict tempo, always yielding to the meaning of the word. Puccini marks copious markings: ritardando, *affrettando*, tenuto, staccato, *portate le voce*, and so on. They are all aids in singing and interpreting the roles, and the coach must help the singer find and perform as many of these as possible.

Though Puccini uses many passages of parlando singing over an orchestral theme, the moments we remember most are the incredibly melodic arias, and there the orchestra shadows the singer in many passages. The long lines of "Che gelida manina" or "Tu, che di gel sei cinta" are accompanied much more completely and heavily than similar moments in Verdi. This makes the high C in *Bohème* relatively easy for the tenor. He has merely to ride the orchestral line-up, not competing with it but enjoying it (far easier than the high C in Gounod's *Faust!*). This melodic doubling, however, invites pushing, and the singer who allows himself to do that will surely fail. But if he keeps a lithe line riding on the orchestral fabric, he can rise comfortably to the heights.

A coach must realize that with Puccini and the verismo school we enter into a kind of open-throated singing that carries with it the emotion of every note and word. Caruso, Del Monaco, Zenatello, Corelli, Tebaldi, Callas, and Taddei are all examples of this kind of totally committed vocalism. The goal is to make an audience think you are giving your all, and yet that can be quite boring ... and dangerous! Mario Del Monaco, noted for a generally *forte* approach to singing, still managed to sing some exquisitely soft passages in *Andrea Chenier* — when he wanted to. It is the coach's job to help singers achieve the passages of tender and softer singing, as this helps them endure throughout an entire role, and it helps them gain in the variety of singing.

I might point out that others in the verismo school — Ruggiero Leoncavallo, Francesco Cilea, Umberto Giordano, and Pietro Mascagni — are sometimes even more overtly dramatic than Puccini, and again the coach must help the singer retain some variety. The all-out approach seems exciting at first, but it then becomes somewhat boring. The fact that Puccini writes in a slightly lower tessitura might make a singer believe the roles are easier or, perhaps, more overtly dramatic. But the singer who allows his or her voice to get "bigger" in the middle voice will find him- or herself fighting hard for effects not intended by the composer.

Puccini and his contemporaries could write some very complicated music when needed. Some of the ensembles in these operas are full of exciting arguments and actions, while some of the atmosphere created by offstage singers, chimes, cannons, and so on, can be difficult and time-consuming to put together. *Gianni Schicchi*, for example, has the ensemble of the relatives being furious at being left out of the will, and the dressing trio can be just as difficult to get right. These kinds of scenes are just as much a part of the whole as the arias and duets we all love.

There is one important thing to note that can help in the interpretation of Puccini. That is the presence of many recordings of first interpreters. Caruso, Farrar, Zenatello, and others were all given premieres by Puccini or were at least trained by him for second or third productions. These give us the best possible connection with exactly what the composer wanted. The fact that Leoncavallo actually accompanied artists in his songs and arias is important. There are even groups of recordings of first casts (Francesco Cilea's *Adrianna Lecouvreur*) and first Met casts (*Madama Butterfly*). The student (or coach) who ignores these recordings because they are not high fidelity and digitally recorded is missing the considerable wealth of nuance these recordings embrace.

13

OPERETTAS

IN THE MID-NINETEENTH CENTURY THE split between grand opera and opéra comique took a new twist. Grand opera was supposed to be in five acts, was to have ballet in the second, third, or fourth acts, was to have no dialogue (*only* recitative), and was to have an historically or biblically based story, with noble causes being sung about. Spectacle, the bigger and more lavish the better, was important, too.

Opéra comique was a more sedate operatic venture. Technically, it was family entertainment. It was usually in three or four acts, had dialogue (with minimal sung recitative that propelled into certain numbers) and little or no ballet (folk-based, if at all), and was to be on a more or less domestic subject. *Daughter of the Regiment, Fra Diavolo* (by Auber), *Faust,* and *Carmen* were written in this form, the latter raising great hackles because of the dramatic content of the story. These styles began to merge into a sort of lyric opera, less grand and more romantically inclined, with fewer historical events and more personal struggles.

In France, along came Jacques Offenbach, an émigré from Germany. His personal style was quite that of a dandy, with lavish suits and shirts and a distinctly "different" manner about him. But he invented a new musical form, which he called opéra bouffe or bouffon. This is nothing more than the French equivalent of opera buffo from Italian. It was

157

terribly funny, quite light, little or no meaning (other than an occasional political barb), and contained pleasant melodies and farcical situations. It was written in two or three acts and had plenty of spoken dialogue to further the action along. Offenbach was equally famous for his one-act comic operas, which he called *operettes*. As the form took root and spread, particularly the Viennese took the name and made it an Italian version of the word: operetta. I might point out that Gilbert and Sullivan, who brought the form to great standards in England, never called their works operettas but rather comic operas (sometimes with modifying phrases specific to certain works).

As anyone who has heard a Gilbert and Sullivan comic opera will know, there are often pages of dialogue, some of it quite funny and some even serious. Though Johann Strauss's *Die Fledermaus* is usually produced with only minimal dialogue between numbers, the original dialogue was quite lengthy and involved. (The opéra comique operas also had long stretches of dialogue, but as most of these are either presented with recitatives today or with the dialogue greatly reduced, we will assume that the lessons learned in this chapter will carry over to that form as well.)

Directors might assume that singers, particularly if they are acting in their own language, can speak dialogue intelligently. It is not necessarily that easy. Dialogue in operettas is filled with parenthetical phrases and asides to the audience. The whole manner is at a higher energy level. What may serve as a reserved and appropriate level for a TV or movie dialogue will seem flat and unimaginative for the operetta character. Characters in operetta may stem from reality — at least somewhat — but they are more overtly limned, more completely above a normal, everyday pace of life. An actor working with operetta dialogue must find the winks and leers in the script and bring them out. Instead of stating a line like "Of course you could do that" in a matter-of-fact fashion, underlining "Of course …," the actor may want to consider other possibilities. "Of course you *could* do that!" or even "Of course, *you* could do that" (implication being "but *I* couldn't"). The practiced operetta actor will take all dialogue and try different readings to find the exact accents that work best. These characters are based in reality but they are not real. They are directly from French farce, and sensible reactions to things are not always assured. One might say characters "pose."

The coach may think that he has nothing to do with dialogue, and in a sense he does not. Yet an understanding of that dialogue is essential because the flavor carries over into the music as well. The most important and dangerous mistake a coach can make is assuming that operetta is "easy" music. Listen to an amateur production of Gilbert and Sullivan or of *Die Fledermaus* and you quickly find out just how precise the music must be, both in musical projection and in dramatic intention.

Some directors rooted in the dramatic schools attempt to get a "better" speaking voice from singers by having them push their speaking voices down in pitch. This eliminates the range, and forces the singer to place their voices in the wrong range. The fact that Beverly Sills sang in a high register and spoke quite low is an isolated anomaly. She is not to be followed. A clearly produced voice, sounding in the middle range, will project quite well and will not have the thin, high sound that directors are trying to avoid. Supporting the speaking voice and projecting it are just as important as the similar efforts in the singing voice.

To project clearly numbers like "Were you not to Ko-Ko plighted" or "I am so proud" from *The Mikado* takes real consideration of vocal, verbal, and technical demands. The technique discussed elsewhere of working patter up to a top speed will of course come into play. But it is also true that dramatic placement of kisses in the first number or of the counterpoint in the second is quite important. These do not just happen, and a coach should insist on rehearsal of whatever is needed to get everything "into" the body. It does not mean that Nanki-Poo and Yum-Yum have to kiss in every rehearsal, but it does mean they should make a physical "kiss" into the air so they know the difficulty of wedging them into place within the prescribed time.

The vocal demands in operetta are sometimes just as great as those demanded in French grand opera and sometimes even greater. An aria like Rosalinde's "Czardas" in *Die Fledermaus* demands the most of any soprano, beginning with a low tessitura and ending with an "effortless" high D. The musical style, though it lands on the listener's ear with pleasant ease, can be quite involved. The only thing lighter is the storyline. The physical demands in dancing and high energy can sap even the experienced performer.

The coach must realize therefore that, when standing still in coaching, singers must concentrate on the physical element of singing with diction. If the singer cannot project the musical and dramatic ideals when standing still, then the coach will realize that more work is necessary. The coach may have to make the singer realize, however, that can-cans, waltzes, and other actions all take energy, and that energy applied to the body takes focus away from the vocal work. If a person has trouble singing an energetic passage standing still, a workout regimen should be recommended.

Coaches must realize the sheer discipline involved in singers performing operetta. The great Gilbert and Sullivan performers of the early 1950s may show some questionable vocalism, but projection of text and the meaning of that text is impeccable and always at the correct energy level. They stand as models of a musical style to be emulated. Those recordings lack dialogue, but the few recordings that have dialogue in them can give a good idea of the style that should be used.

NOTE: It has become a recent development with companies that they produce operas with spoken dialogue in English and the musical numbers sung in German or French. This is not an ideal situation. It is true that it retains the correct words in the music, and that the drama comes through more clearly in the vernacular. But it always seems to say that singers are able to sing a language but unable to speak it. It is also quite a jolt when a character like Dr. Falke (in *Die Fledermaus*) is speaking quite naturally in English and then lapses into an equally conversational tone in German. It just seems wrong somehow. And in more serious works like Weber's *Der Freischütz*, the jolt can be even more extreme. How can one take seriously the following exchange?

> *Agathe*: Where did you shoot the deer?
>
> *Max*:   Somewhat far from here — deep in the woods — in the Wolf's Glen.

No. 9 Terzett   *Agathe*: Wie? Was? Entsetzen!

> Dort in der Schreckensschlucht?
>
> Dort — in der Schreckensschlucht?

She is literally answering one word with the roughly the same word in German. It seems like a good idea on paper, but the constant shift from one language to another is quite upsetting, and I do not recommend the experiment. I am not alone, I think, since the practice seems to be fading.

14

BENJAMIN BRITTEN AND OTHER MODERN COMPOSERS

MANY COMPOSERS WANT TO WRITE operas, and yet they despair because singers do not seem to want to sing their works. The composer cannot understand the reluctance of the singers, while the singers fire back that composers just do not understand the needs of opera. Both are accurate to a degree.

Singers are generally raised in a school of singing that fits the works of the Italian or French composers. Some adapt themselves for German and Russian operas, and some even manage a few English-language operas. There is an English school that embraces the Handelian oratorio (but not necessarily his operas) and the operatic works of Britten, Vaughan William, and Delius. But very few singers are taught a technique that will enable them to tackle the many works that have been written since 1940. That date would hardly seem to qualify an opera as a "modern opera" in an historian's eyes, but to a singer it does. Even Britten has only gradually gained ground. The other composers are interpreted by a select few singers, like Sanford Sylvan, who seem to specialize in the modern works and relish the demands they present.

The fact is that many modern operas are story-oriented, which is to say that they present a decidedly plot-formed opera, and the various characters may have little dramatic time to develop. Other operas may be just the opposite, with developed characters but no story to take those characters anywhere. And some operas have so much "conversation" that nothing happens. *Peter Grimes* has wonderful characters that live and breathe in a fashion that would interest any singer. But even later Britten operas have not gained prominence, and this is in part because those operas are not populated with characters that are of really abiding interest.

The other pressing problem for singers is the sheer difficulty of learning a modern opera. A singer might be able to learn a Puccini or Verdi opera in a few weeks, but an opera by Henze, Adams, Adamo, or Previn will take much longer, involving considerable "woodshedding" to learn notes and rhythms. Even works that are tonal and seemingly straightforward may actually involve considerable effort to learn.

It is one thing for a singer to sing some of the works "correctly" with music in front of him or her, and it is quite another thing to invest the character with feelings and attitudes, at the same time singing the whole opera correctly from memory. And after all of the effort to learn the work, how many other productions will the singer be asked to do of that opera? The answer, unfortunately, is very few.

Benjamin Britten, Aaron Copland, Dominick Argento, Douglas Moore, and Carlyle Floyd all present similar difficulties, although their styles are really quite different. Whether overtly British (in Britten) or clearly American (the others), these composers share a tonality-based style, with text setting quite natural for the regions represented by the stories. In all cases, certain regional accents may be appropriate and desired. This may be as important to these scores as Viennese slang dialect is for Baron Ochs in *Der Rosenkavalier* by Strauss. Such accents, however, may elicit vocal responses that clearly pull the voice out of line. The coach will have to develop a good ear both for accents and vocal placement and line. The Southern American "twang" from the back of the throat is not appropriate for good singing, even if it is appropriate for certain characters in American operas.

In these composers, the vocal writing can frequently be centered in the middle voice. The music is based on a more episodic, rhapsodic flow of music and not on forms. This means that arias do not unfold with ABA or AAB as in earlier composers. Themes may return and develop, but that does not say that they are set in a formal way. Duets and whole scenes can unfold as dramatically driven, the music reinforcing the scene structure and not a musical format.

If, as in Floyd's *Susannah*, Copland's *The Tender Land,* or Britten's *Peter Grimes*, a dance is used for a dramatic device, the folk element of that dance will dictate the music and possibly the vocal element with the dance, but the dramatic flow will not be dictated by traditional aria forms.

Rhythms are usually more obtuse than in the earlier composers (other than possibly Richard Strauss). The correct rhythmic performance of each line may be quite important. An ensemble such as the Threnody from act 3 of *Albert Herring* by Britten must be rehearsed many times to make it totally live as an ensemble. Similarly, the earlier Handelian excess at the close of the first scene of that opera must be carefully rehearsed for tonal reasons and for rhythmic precision.

The recitative passages in these composers can be quite varied. Some composers continue the line begun as far back as Donizetti, with a continuous music underpinning the vocal lines, while other composers, like Britten in *Albert Herring* and Stravinsky in *The Rake's Progress*, adopt a form of secco recitative to great effect.

Those composers listed above are considered conservative. But never underestimate the difficulty of making those composers come alive. Some scenes may require a keen ear and rhythmic sense. Barber's *Vanessa* is quite difficult to sing correctly and dramatically. The text, by Menotti, is purposefully obtuse and unclear, but that only adds to the gothic overtones of the piece.

Floyd's *Of Mice and Men* has some scenes, such as the scene in which Lennie murders Curly's Wife, which are frightening, fascinating, pathetic, and very moving — all at the same time.

Gian-Carlo Menotti, of course, wrote not only the text for *Vanessa*, but he also composed quite a few operas himself. His style has been described as post-Puccini, though that is an oversimplification of the facts. In his best works: *The Telephone, The Medium, Amelia al Ballo, The Old Maid and the Thief,* and *Amahl and the Night Visitors,* he creates music and texts that resonate perfectly together and give singers a lot to work with. In his lesser works, notably those of later vintage, he seems to be working through stale territory. His dramatic impetus, once so keen and strong, faded as he approached the 1960s. The potency of those early operas listed, however, should be noted, and coaches will be dealing with arias and scenes from them for a long time. They are classics, just as are works by Verdi, and coaches must put in just as much care and understanding (and be just as strong with singers, who sing incorrectly or with no care with the text) as they do with the "greater" masters.

If the list of composers already given could be said to be an extension of traditional writing, Hans Werner Henze is a jump to a more difficult style of vocal writing. *Elegy for Young Lovers* is quite fabulous to see, the intensity of the drama taking hold of an audience and moving it quite beyond expectations. But the difficulty of learning an opera like that or the same composer's *Der junge Lord* (The young lord) is extreme. First is the range/tessituras of some of the roles, high notes liberally reaching the upper limits. There is a wide usage of vocal tricks (*Sprechstimme*, sotto voce, *tonlos*, etc.) and the silences become quite lengthy and important. But most daunting is the harmonic language, nontonal in its basis and very reflective of the emotional state of the characters.

That scenes from the operas mentioned can come across dramatically and musically usually means that the singers have worked very hard to assimilate the music and get inside the characters. The best modern operas have interesting characters. Composers should realize that such characters make the learning difficulties all worthwhile. Those operas that are only story-driven are possibly a little too bland to arouse interest, whether those operas are modern or from the bel canto era.

Here it would be well to address the problem of tessitura versus range. Few composers write beyond the range of a given voice type, because they look them up in a book and stay within the parameters given. A range is simply the scope of a role from highest note to lowest. Tessitura deals with where within that range most of the notes lie. Rodolfo in *La Bohème* (Puccini) and Faust in *Faust* (Gounod) have exactly the same range, but the tessitura in Faust is about a second higher than Rodolfo. Hoffmann (Offenbach), though lacking the high C, is much higher than either. Too many composers write either too low (afraid to tax the singer) or too high, not realizing that a singer can no more sustain a constantly high tessitura than can a trumpeter or hornist.

Other extremes exist in "modern" composers. John Adams and Philip Glass are relatively tonal, but their usage of minimalism and difficult rhythms makes learning time quite long. The singers must be mathematicians to keep in mind the shifting repetitions.

William Bolcom writes in an immediately approachable idiom that belies some of the carefully worked-out structure.

André Previn's only performed opera to date has been *A Streetcar Named Desire*, but his approach captures the decadent and rather jazzy element of New Orleans quite well, and the opera has taken off with several productions scattered around the world.

Henry Mollicone has also had several major operas given, most important being *The Face on the Barroom Floor* and *Coyote Tales*. These are mainly tonal, stylistically leaning somewhat toward a more popular style of singing.

These composers use almost as many varied approaches to composition as there are composers. The coach must find the style and make the singer aware of what it takes to put the music across. Unlike with older composers, few recordings of modern operas exist (though these are usually conducted by the composer). So the old-fashioned method of painstakingly learning the notes and rhythms from scratch from the printed page is the only adequate way to learn the music. And for this most singers will definitely need a coach.

One of the first questions the singer will have will concern the rhythm, because such rhythms do not come easily, even though they are "natural." Notes and rhythms in modern scores reflect the correct inflection to an extent not considered by the nineteenth-century composers. This "natural" way of singing sometimes actually takes more time than the stanzas of earlier operas. The learning of rhythms and pitches must come almost simultaneously with the study of the dramatic projection, because they are so completely and intrinsically linked. One solution is to speak the words in rhythm and tempo. At this stage, it is best to take small sections at a time. After this task is mastered, the singer should add "melodic" contours. The most natural inflections should be sought, with careful consideration of the dramatic thought behind each line or situation. Other things, such as jazz rhythms, may affect the rhythms as well. Even "easier" modern composers such as Gian-Carlo Menotti will require effort on certain passages.

The second question will be: "How do I find that pitch?" The coach must point out the methods possible. Few composers leave a singer without some related pitch somewhere to find their notes. The excerpts found in the chapter on Wagner and Strauss show how even these earlier composers could have pitches difficult to find and to sing. A voice, unlike a clarinet or trumpet, has no set place for a pitch; it is not a matter of fingering and embouchure. (Not all composers understand this, and they write with no consideration for the vocalist finding a pitch.) Except in those singers with perfect pitch, they do not have a fixed placement for a given pitch. Even if a singer may develop a good sense of relative pitch, they cannot pull tonal centers out of thin air. And some people with "perfect pitch" will tell you it is not really "perfect" either.

The coach needs to find ways for the singer to relate to the music. It may involve interval relationships to the music heard, or it may involve the understanding of mini-tonal centers. Even obtuse intervals may be found in this way. It is not best to try to learn the pitches by rote, because an aural stimulus can easily throw the singer off. At the premiere of *Bomarzo* by Ginastera, obscure pitches were reportedly found by having instrumentalists standing just offstage playing them for the various singers. This is *not* recommended. (The singers in question were experienced opera singers, too!)

It is far better if the coach can help the singer hear the pitches in the orchestral underpinning, getting them to understand the harmonic structure over or in which they are singing.

Combining the approaches in this way, the notes come slowly but surely, and the rhythms become firmly entrenched because they are related to the totality. One might call this going beyond the obvious. The task of singing notes and rhythms, so difficult in and of itself, now becomes only the first step toward the ultimate goal: a complete realization of the character through all of the symbols left by the composer.

The coach and director may have to explain the dramatic structure of the opera or character — in post-Freudian works that means that the operas lean heavily on the psychological element. Gone are the poses some great characters seemed to take, replaced by the intuitive and probing sense of the character. It may also mean structures in which traditional narrative approaches are forsaken.

This means that coaches must understand modern drama almost as much as modern opera. So the coach who is content to work on dynamics and other strictly musical things is not fulfilling the needs of the singer.

And, of course, the coach must learn to play the piano reductions as best he can. There are many problems with this. As expressed elsewhere, coaches sometimes have to rewrite the piano-vocal score just to be able to negotiate the tricky ways of reduction. Important lines may be given to hands that are crossed, or lines may be octave-transposed. Sometimes orchestral rhythms may be so at odds with one another that one brain and pair of hands can't reproduce it all. It may also be a fact that the coach (and singer) is working from a photocopy of a manuscript page. (This objectionable problem is understandable, however, since really printing it out sets in stone music that may be changed in rehearsals. Modern computers are helping to change this problem.) It is amazing how difficult these modern works can be to read. It may involve figuring out how to play a given passage — or it may involve figuring out the composer's intentions for that same passage. What seems clear to a composer at one point can be quite obtuse to a coach or conductor when the composer is not around to explain.

Opera has even entered the aleatoric arena, where the order of certain musical events may be dictated, but the exact length or pitches of those events may vary. This takes yet another kind of patience and expertise. A coach and singers may be tempted to laugh at some of the "silly" things composers request, but since the performance still looms, it serves no one's goals.

In the areas discussed in the chapters so far, this need for patient and careful study is the most comprehensive and difficult area of the working process to pin down due to the extremely wide variety of approaches to the problem of composing opera. It makes the growing awareness of operas of our time even more special. Mainstream singers are starting to consider these operas more and more. But they are also surveying the unusual repertoire from all of the other composers, too. Handel revivals are on a par with those of works by Britten or Moore. Early or unexplored Verdi, Rossini, and Wagner are finding their ways to the stage almost as frequently as some of the "standard" works. Singers will always find works rewarding if they are able to create good characters and sing music that has interest and color. These are what make learning new music viable and interesting. These are the goals. The coach who can understand the technical difficulties and help singers to get through them and to find the goal is a well-respected and valuable coach for any singer to know. That coach must help the singer establish a system with which to learn new kinds of rhythms and characters. The study of modern operas makes the singer learn without the usage of recordings (because they probably do not exist), and that helps them develop "chops" for learning any music more quickly and more accurately. More and more new operas are being premiered almost weekly, and coaches must be able to analyze the difficulties in a score and proceed with a singer based on that analysis.

Systematic working through a score involves taking each step in learning carefully. The singer and coach can work out the best method with which to attack a problematic score. For some scores it is best to take the rhythms first, divorced from accompaniment and pitches, adding the sung pitches only after rhythm has been mastered. Adding the accompaniment may take several steps alone (bass line, chords, simplified figures from the accompaniment). It can take an entire hour of coaching to work through one relatively small scene. But, as with the passagework in the florid singing of bel canto operas, learning the music carefully and correctly first negates a lot of problems that arise when such care is not taken. Passages like the one found in the middle of Albert's great act 2 monologue of *Albert Herring* — "Dish after dish they brought us ..." — must be exactly in tempo, inflected "naturally" and made to fly from the mind and lips of the singer.

A scene like the opening scene from Berg's *Wozzeck* is quite difficult for the Captain. His angular vocal line is all over the vocal range,

168 • Opera Coaching

verbally pointed and filled with tricky rhythms. Yet, when done properly, the effect is positively maniacal. His vocal line alone solves most of the problems of characterization.

But Berg and Britten are hardly modern composers. The most modern composers are sometimes easier by the measure, but the accumulative difficulties of changing rhythms or repeated rhythms (in minimalism) are sometimes tricky to learn and disconcertingly awkward to "feel." Modern singers must develop the memory and musical chops for these new scores. Haphazard learning of such music leads to major headaches in rehearsals. Since it doesn't seem that modern composers will ever return to a simpler style of writing (I'm not really suggesting that they do so), it is incumbent on the singers to improve their abilities. The new operas like Mark Adamo's *Little Women* and *Lysistrata* or John Corigliano's *The Ghosts of Versailles* are so rewarding that singers can benefit from developing such learning "chops" and gain the really wonderful characters in their repertoire.

INTERLUDE SEVEN

OPERA IN TRANSLATION

In the United States we like to think of ourselves as, at one time at least, being at odds with the world, in that we used to perform a great many of our operas in English. This is not as odd as it seems. As late as the early 1970s, German and Italian opera houses the size of the Hamburgische Staatsoper or La Scala still performed operas in translation.

The Metropolitan even performed the Russian and other Slavic operas in translation later than that. Then, in order to capitalize on international singers and their reputations, companies switched to original language. Colleges have even begun preparing students for this trend by using original language instead of vernacular productions. But there will always continue to be some opera in translation. Comedies in particular lose a great deal if the humor has to be read in the supertitles. Those projected titles do not allow the singer to be less expressive or less specific in their dramatic projection, and diction must still be a major concern.

A coach must help singers deal with the "wrong" words being sung. Good translations place the important words in the same locations (or nearly) and use similar expressions. Some other translations, however, become very freewheeling and distant from the original libretto. This is not as terrible as it seems. Some verbal idioms are not translatable exactly into English. An easy example to demonstrate this is in a dialogue from *Die Zauberflöte*. At the entrance of the Queen of the Night in act 2, Monostatos, seeing that Pamina is her daughter, declares,

"Das ist Salz in meine Suppe." That means literally, "That's salt in my soup/stew." But that means nothing to us in English. An idiomatic equivalent might be, "That's a feather in my cap."

The first difficult problem in singing in translation is that words are displaced from one part of a phrase to another, which means coloration devices of the composer might fall inaccurately on the wrong words. Sometimes this just cannot be avoided. It must sound like English, not some odd translation. For example: If the words so backward fall that they English resemble not to anyone, then the translation not good is (as this sentence shows). A translation should not sound like a bad imitation of Yoda in the famous *Star Wars* movies. Some arias, like "V'adoro pupille" from Handel's *Giulio Cesare*, are virtually untranslatable in anything like an accurate singing text.

In making translations, it is sometimes quite difficult to get the best phrasing and meaning into the given notes. An example is found in *Die Fledermaus*. In the famous solo and chorus from act 2, "Brüderlein und Schwesterlein" literally mean "little brother and little sister." But that does not fit the few notes given. In my translation, I actually began the verse with, "All of you, each and every one of you …" It dealt with the situation at hand and allowed the articulation to be ultralegato. It is not the only solution, but it had virtues that outweighed the faults. I reverted to "brother dear, brother dear and sister, too" at the repeat of the phrase two lines later.

Another problem with singing in translation is the vowels. Some words translate closely but with vastly different sounds. Herz, cor, coeur, and heart all mean the same thing, but what a difference the various vowels make. The astute coach may have to adjust a translation for a singer just because he or she needs a different vowel on a high note. This is awkward, of course, because a translation has been paid for and usually should be followed quite closely. But some adjustment is made in almost every performance. Coaches should make suggestions with a cautious warning that some conductors and directors will not allow deviations from the sung or spoken text. Even if the coach can devise an excellent solution that fits the notes and is twice as literal in meaning, there may be good reasons why changes cannot be made. Adjusting the underlay may help.

Ideally, such changes should not cause major headaches — assuming they are done well and with care. Rhyme schemes must frequently be observed and close meanings need to be attempted. Humorous content is sometimes much more difficult to adjust than the dramatic. Of course some of the older translations become laughable to us because they have really antiquated language. As Tito Gobbi once observed on the Bell Telephone Hour, however, the old librettos of Donizetti and his era are just as flowery and antiquated to the modern Italian ear. So care must be taken. Translation is never an ideal situation, but it can be far preferable to having a singer singing (or speaking) unintelligibly in a foreign tongue, with no discernable meaning emerging. And audiences still respond to the immediacy of hearing their own language in a performance.

What makes a bad translation may be surmised from the above. It is astonishing how distant some translations are from the original-language text. Singers of Prince Orlofsky in *Die Fledermaus* are frequently asked to sing "humorous" texts that sound dated almost as soon as they are written, yet the original text of his aria paints a picture of a spoiled autocrat so well, you wonder why the "translator" does not try for a closer rendering of the text. Nemorinos in *L'Elisir d'amore* are sometimes asked to sing terrible vowels throughout "Una furtiva lagrima," and again they stray rather far from the original. It is sometimes a matter of taste, but a coach should practice the art of making singing translations. They will learn a lot about the verbal end of their work.

Some operas, of course, suffer greatly when translated. *Pélleas et Mélisande* provides an ideal example. In addition to being quintessentially French — musically, verbally, dramatically, and idealogically — it has phrases that just do not translate into easy phrases. Take Mélisande's first phrase. She sings "Ne me touché pas" several times in succession. It means simply, "Don't touch me." But that does not fit the number of notes given. One can try again and again to make a singing translation, but anything one tries will come up several notches below the easy flow of the original. This and the aforementioned *Giulio Cesare* of Handel can provide hours of frustration to any translator.

Another test: Secco recitatives should end in a rhymed couplet. Most translators just skip that aspect and hope for a good closing line with meaning that does not rhyme. Translating is a great skill, and the question will always be raised whether singing the "wrong" words is a good practice or not.

15

CONCLUSIONS

BASED ON THE AMOUNT OF information considered in the preceding pages, the idea of becoming an opera coach might seem an insurmountable hurdle. Opera is so vast an area (ranging from 1600 to the present) that the idea of encompassing all of these genres is daunting in the extreme. Certainly no book can hope to encompass all of the considerations necessary for any style or practice. But the repertoire is really rather slimmer than that. It embraces really only about fifty to seventy-five operas, with the others existing in the fringes through arias and ensembles. For example, a coach might do well at some point to learn the closing aria from *Capriccio* by Richard Strauss, but the chances of coaching that opera complete are far fewer. One might very well expect to find *Salome, Elektra, Der Rosenkavalier,* and *Ariadne auf Naxos* on an opera company's plan. Even *Arabella* has really only come into its own in the last decade or two.

The important thing is that a coach gains the understanding of how to put together an opera, how to coach it, and how to make a singer come alive in a role. It is always possible to learn a new opera. In fact most opera coaches will say that they have strange blanks in their repertoire of operas that have just never come their way. For example, unless a coach is working for a major opera house, he or she will probably not have the opportunity to work with complete works of Wagner or the grander operas of Verdi. Still they must understand the style, because scenes and arias will most certainly appear from time to time. And working in the larger houses will most certainly involve those masters.

The study of piano leads generally to one repertoire. The wider study of chamber music or accompanying give the pianist the awareness of a broad range of music and techniques never encountered in solo music. Opera expands that realm even further.

If knowledge of languages is an added plus in other music, it is a necessity in the study of operatic works. If sensitivity to phrasing and dynamics is important in solo works and chamber music, they grow greatly in importance when confronted by the demands and scope of opera. There are even works like Brahm's *Liebeslieder Waltzes* (vocal quartet and piano duet) that pianists are asked to play on occasion, and the rehearsals for those will be, basically, coaching sessions, in which words and phrasing, balances, and tempi are all worked out together, quite like working out ensembles in operas. No two coaches are exactly alike in these endeavors either. Each coach develops his or her methods and techniques, building up an idea of how best to approach each problem that comes along.

All of these things the opera coach can approach and learn. It is not a wild plethora of unrelated facts, but it is instead an interconnected chain that has grown and spread from the single first opera in 1600 to encompass various reactions to the single word: "opera" (plural for "opus," which means work).

The job of a coach must include analysis of what makes a particular piece of music difficult — dramatically, musically, technically, or even physically. No one will tell a singer more effectively what makes a role difficult than a coach. A coach who approaches this field with an inquisitive mind and enthusiasm will find it is a field with many rewards and, yes, with many difficulties. But the difficulties are all worth the effort in the final analysis, and those rewards will make all the efforts seem trivial.

APPENDIX A

A LIST OF VOCAL *FACHS* AND THEIR ROLES

THE FOLLOWING LIST IS EXTENSIVE *but not exhaustive. There are sure to be some omissions. Some roles might also fit into more than one category or might be cast in different ways in different productions. This is simply a list as prescribed by the German opera houses. Some roles have changed their casting since this list was written out for me, and some have changed in our perceptions of them in the last twenty years or so. It is a guide with real merit, but it is not infallible, and some will actually disagree with it. I have included some roles not generally performed in Germany in the interest of being as complete as possible. Those listed without arias have much to sing, but no excerpts.*

COLORATURA SOPRANO

Ariadne auf Naxos	R. Strauss	Zerbinetta	"Groß mächtige Prinzessin"
Un Ballo in Maschera	Verdi	Oscar	two arias
Il Barbiere di Siviglia (also considered a coloratura mezzo role)	Rossini	Rosina	"Una voce poca fa"
La Bohème	Puccini	Musetta	"Quando m'en vo"
Les Contes d'Hoffmann	Offenbach	Olympia	"Les oiseaux"
Entführung aus dem Serail	Mozart	Constanza	three arias
Faust	Gounod	Marguerite	"Roi de Thule"/"Air di Bijoux"
Lakmé	Delibes	Lakmé	"Bell Song"
Lucia di Lammermoor	Donizetti	Lucia	"Regnava nel silenzio"/Mad Scene
Lustigen Weiber von Windsor	Nicolai	Frau Fluth	"Nun eilt herbei"
Manon	Massenet	Manon	three arias
Pagliacci	Leoncavallo	Nedda	"Stridono lassu"
I Puritani	Bellini	Elvira	"Qui la voce"
Rigoletto	Verdi	Gilda	"Caro nome"
Roméo et Juliette	Gounod	Juliette	Juliette's Waltz

La Traviata	Verdi	Violetta	"Ah, forse lui"/ "Sempre libera" + "Addio del passato"

(also cast as a lyric soprano)

Die Zauberflöte	Mozart	Königin	"O zittre nicht"/"Der hölle Rache"

SOUBRETTE

Arabella	R. Strauss	Zdenka	no aria

(could be a lyric or even coloratura soprano)

Cosi fan Tutte	Mozart	Despina	"In uomini"/"Una donna"
Don Giovanni	Mozart	Zerlina	"Batti, batti"/"Vedrai carino"
Don Pasquale	Donizetti	Norina	"So anch'io la virtu magica"
L'Elisir d'amore	Donizetti	Adina	"Prendi"
Entführung aus dem Serail	Mozart	Blonde	two arias
Fidelio	Beethoven	Marzellina	"O wär ich schon mit dir vereint"
La Fille du Régiment	Donizetti	Marie	three arias
Die Fledermaus	J. Strauss	Adele	"Mein Herr, Marquis"
Der Freischütz	Weber	Ännchen	"Kommt ein schlanker Bursch gegangen"
Gianni Schicchi	Puccini	Lauretta	"O mio babbino caro"
Hänsel und Gretel	Humperdinck	Gretel	"Awakening Aria"
Die Lustigen Weiber	Nicolai	Anna	one aria
Le Nozze di Figaro	Mozart	Susanna	two arias
Der Rosenkavalier	R. Strauss	Sophie	act 2 duet/act 3 trio
Werther	Massenet	Sophie	two arias

LYRIC SOPRANO

Arabella	R. Strauss	Arabella	"Schluß"
The Bartered Bride	Smetana	Mařenka (Marie)	two arias
La Bohème	Puccini	Mimi	"Mi chiamano Mimi"/ "Donde lieta usci"
Carmen	Bizet	Micaela	"Je dis que rien ne m'épouvante"
Cosi fan tutte	Mozart	Fiordiligi	"Come scoglio"/"Per pieta"
Don Giovanni	Mozart	Donna Elvira	three arias
Elektra	R. Strauss	Chrysothemis	no real arias
Die Fledermaus	J. Strauss	Rosalinde	Czardas
Der Freischütz	Weber	Agathe	"Leise, leise"/"Und ob die Wolke"
Guillaume Tell	Rossini	Mathilde	"Sombre forêt" ("Selva opaca")
Idomeneo	Mozart	Ilia	three arias
Manon Lescaut	Puccini	Manon	"In quelle trini morbide"/ "Sola, perduta"
Le Nozze di Figaro	Mozart	Countess	"Porgi amor"/"Dove sono"
Otello	Verdi	Desdemona	"Salce, salce"/"Ave Maria"
Susannah	Floyd	Susannah	"Ain't it a pretty night"/ "The trees on the mountains"

Turandot	Puccini	Liù	"Signore, ascolta"/ "Tu, che di gel sei cinta"
Vanessa	Barber	Vanessa	"Do not utter a word, Anatol"
Der Wildschütz	Lortzing	Baronin	one aria
Yevghenyi Onegin	Tchaikovsky	Tatiana	Letter Scene
Die Zauberflöte	Mozart	Pamina	"Ach, ich fühl's"

DRAMATIC AND HOCH-DRAMATIC SOPRANO

Aïda	Verdi	Aïda	"Ritorna vincitor"/"O Patria mia"
Andrea Chenier	Giordano	Maddalena	"La Mamma morta"
Antony and Cleopatra	Barber	Cleopatra	two arias
Ariadne auf Naxos	R. Strauss	Ariadne	"Es gibt ein Reich"
Un Ballo in Maschera	Verdi	Amelia	two arias
Don Carlos	Verdi	Elizabeth	two arias
Don Giovanni	Mozart	Donna Anna	"Or sai chi l'onore"/"Non mi dir"

(Also considered a lyric or dramatic-coloratura)

Elektra	R. Strauss	Elektra	"Agamemnon"
Fidelio	Beethoven	Leonore	"Abscheulicher"
Der Fliegende Holländer	Wagner	Senta	one aria
La Forza del Destino	Verdi	Leonora	two arias
Lohengrin	Wagner	Elsa	"Elsa's Traum"
Madama Butterfly	Puccini	Butterfly	"Un bel di vedremo"/"Tu, tu, tu, piccolo addio"

(can also be placed in the lyric soprano category)

Die Meistersinger von Nürnberg	Wagner	Eva	"Sachs, mein Freund"
Norma	Bellini	Norma	"Casta diva"

(This role is particularly difficult to place in any *Fach*.)

Ring Cycle	Wagner		
Die Walküre		Sieglinde	"Die Männer Sippe"/"Du bist der Lenz"
Die Walküre		Brünnhilde	"Hojotoho"
Siegfried		Brünnhilde	"Ewig war ich"
Die Götterdämmerung		Brünnhilde	Immolation Scene
Der Rosenkavalier	R. Strauss	Marschallin	two arias
Rusalka	Dvořák	Rusalka	"Moon Aria"
Salome	R. Strauss	Salome	Final Scene
Tannhäuser	Wagner	Elizabeth	"Dich teure Halle"/"Gebet"
Tosca	Puccini	Tosca	"Vissi d'arte"
Tristan und Isolde	Wagner	Isolde	Narration and Curse/"Liebestod"
Il Trovatore	Verdi	Leonora	two arias
Turandot	Puccini	Turandot	"In questa reggia"

DRAMATIC MEZZO-SOPRANO AND ALTO

Aïda	Verdi	Amneris	Judgment Scene
Ariadne auf Naxos	R. Strauss	Componist	"Sein wird wieder gut"
Un Ballo in Maschera	Verdi	Ulrica	Incantation Scene

Carmen	Bizet	Carmen	Habanera, Seguidilla, and Card Scene
Cavalleria Rusticana	Mascagni	Santuzza	"Voi lo sapete, o Mamma"

(Though listed for and often sung by sopranos, this role is frequently taken by mezzos.)

Don Carlos	Verdi	Eboli	"Veil Aria"/"O Don Fatale"
Khovanschina	Mussorgsky	Marfa	"Night Song"
Lohengrin	Wagner	Ortrud	Curse
Macbeth	Verdi	Lady Macbeth	three arias

(See note on *Cavalleria Rusticana*.)

Orfeo ed Euridice	Gluck	Orfeo	"Che faro, senza Euridice"
Orleanskaya Dieva	Tchaikovsky	Joan	"Adieu Forêt"

(This opera also goes by the titles *Maid of Orleans* and *Joan of Arc*.)

Parsifal	Wagner	Kundry	"Ich sah das Kind"

(See note on *Cavalleria Rusticana*.)

Ring Cycle	Wagner		
Rheingold		Erda	"Weiche, Wotan, Weiche"
Die Walküre		Fricka	Scene with Wotan
Götterdämmerung		Waltraute	Narrative
Der Rosenkavalier	R. Strauss	Octavian	Beginning act 1/Rose Duet
Rusalka	Dvořák	Jezibaba	no aria
Samson et Dalila	Saint-Saëns	Dalila	three arias
Tristan und Isolde	Wagner	Brangäne	Brangäne's Watch
Il Trovatore	Verdi	Azucena	two arias
Werther	Massenet	Charlotte	"Letter Aria"/"Va, laisse couler mes larmes"

LYRIC MEZZO-SOPRANO

Il Barbiere di Siviglia	Rossini	Rosina	"Una voce poco fa"
Boris Godunov	Mussorgsky	Marina	Aria/Duet with Dmitri
La Cenerentola	Rossini	Angelina (Cenerentola)	"Non piu mesta"
La Clemenza di Tito	Mozart	Sesto	"Parto, parto"
Cosi fan Tutte	Mozart	Dorabella	two arias
Die Fledermaus	J. Strauss	Orlovsky	"Chacun à son goùt"
Giulio Cesare	Handel	Cesare	various arias
L'Italiana in Algieri	Rossini	Isabella	two arias
Le Nozze di Figaro	Mozart	Cherubino	"Non so piu"/"Voi che sapete"
Vanessa	Barber	Erica	"Must the winter come so soon?"

COUNTERTENOR

El Niño	John Adams	three roles	several ensembles
Giulio Cesare	Handel	Tolomeo	several arias
Orfeo ed Euridice	Gluck	Orfeo	"Che farò, senza Euridice"
A Midsummer Night's Dream	Britten	Oberon	"I know a bank"

(Numerous roles in Handel, Scarlatti, Vivaldi, and other Baroque operas. Recently, composers have begun writing for this category, as in the Adams. Steven Rickards, a member of the original cast of the Adams, is publishing an exhaustive catalogue of works written since 1900 for countertenor.)

LYRIC TENOR (INCLUDING LEGGIERO)

Il Barbiere di Siviglia	Rossini	Almaviva	"Ecco ridente"
La Bohème	Puccini	Rodolfo	"Che gelida manina"
Cenerentola	Rossini	Ramiro	"Principe più non sei"
Cosi fan Tutte	Mozart	Ferrando	three arias
Don Giovanni	Mozart	Don Ottavio	two arias
Don Pasquale	Donizetti	Ernesto	"Povero Ernesto"/"Come gentil"
L'Elisir d'amore	Donizetti	Nemorino	"Quanto è bella"/ "Una furtiva lagrima"
Entführung aus dem Serail	Mozart	Belmonte	four arias
Falstaff	Verdi	Fenton	Opening of act 3
L'Italiana in Algeri	Rossini	Lindoro	two arias
Lustigen Weiber von Windsor	Nicolai	Fenton	"Horch, die Lerche"
I Puritani	Bellini	Arturo	two arias
Rigoletto	Verdi	Duca	"Questa o quella"/"Parmi veder"/ "La donna è mobile"
Der Rosenkavalier	R. Strauss	Italian Tenor	"Di rigori armato"
La Traviata	Verdi	Alfredo	"De miei bolenti spiriti"
Die Zauberflöte	Mozart	Tamino	"Dies Bildnis"/"Flute Aria"

SPINTO TENOR

The Bartered Bride	Smetana	Jeník (Hans)	one aria
Carmen	Bizet	Don José	"La fleur que tu m'avais jetée"
Les Contes d'Hoffmann	Offenbach	Hoffmann	four arias
Faust	Gounod	Faust	"Salut demeure"
Guillaume Tell	Rossini	Arnold(o)	"Asil hérèditaire" ("O muto asil")
Lucia di Lammermoor	Donizetti	Edgardo	"Fra poco a me ricovero"
Madama Butterfly	Puccini	Pinkerton	three arias
Manon	Massenet	Des Grieux	"Le Rève"/"Ah, fuyez douce image"
Tosca	Puccini	Cavaradossi	two arias
Yevghenyi Onegin	Tchaikovsky	Lenski	"Kuda, kuda"

BUFFO TENOR (SPIEL TENOR)

Ariadne auf Naxos	R. Strauss	Tanzmeister/Brighella	one aria
The Bartered Bride	Smetana	Vašek (Wenzel)	two arias
Les Contes d'Hoffmann	Offenbach	Franz (Four Grotesques)	one aria
Entführung aus dem Serail	Mozart	Pedrillo	"Serenade"/"Frisch zum Kampfe"
Hänsel und Gretel	Humperdinck	Die Hexe	one aria
Meistersinger von Nürnberg	Wagner	David	(act 1) "Mein Herr, der Singer"
Le Nozze di Figaro	Mozart	Basilio	"In quegli'anni in cui val poco"
Yeghenyi Onegin	Tchaikovsky	Triquet	"Ah, cette fête conviez"
Die Zauberflöte	Mozart	Monostatos	one aria

DRAMATIC TENOR AND HELDEN TENOR

Aïda	Verdi	Radames	"Celeste Aïda"
Andrea Chenier	Giordano	Andrea Chenier	three arias
Un Ballo in Maschera	Verdi	Riccardo (Gustavo)	two arias
Boris Godunov	Mussorgsky	Dmitri	Garden Aria
Cavalleria Rusticana	Mascagni	Turiddu	two arias
Don Carlos	Verdi	Don Carlos	(one aria, but two versions)
Fidelio	Beethoven	Florestan	"Gott, welch Dunkel hier"
Der Fliegende Holländer	Wagner	Erik	one aria
Der Freischütz	Weber	Max	"Durch die Wälder"
Lohengrin	Wagner	Lohengrin	two arias
Meistersinger von Nürnberg	Wagner	Walther	three arias
Otello	Verdi	Otello	three arias
Pagliacci	Leoncavallo	Canio	three arias
Parsifal	Wagner	Parsifal	"Amfortas"
Ring Cycle	Wagner		
Das Rheingold		Loge	Narrative
Die Walküre		Siegmund	"Ein Schwert/ Winterstürme"
Siegfried		Siegfried	Forging Song
Götterdämmerung		Siegfried	one aria
Tannhäuser	Wagner	Tannhäuser	Rome Narrative
Il Trovatore	Verdi	Manrico	"Ah si, ben mio"/"Di quella pira"
Turandot	Puccini	Calaf	"Non piangere Liù"/"Nessun dorma"

LYRIC BARITONE

Ariadne auf Naxos	R. Strauss	Harlekin	no real aria
Il Barbiere di Siviglia	Rossini	Figaro	"Largo al factotum"
Cenerentola	Rossini	Dandini	"Come un ape"
Cosi fan Tutte	Mozart	Guglielmo	"Non siate ritrosi"/"Donna mie la fate"

(The aria "Rivolgete a lui lo squardo" is occasionally inserted now, but it was withdrawn by Mozart himself and is not really part of the role.)

Don Giovanni	Mozart	Don Giovanni	three arias

(may also be sung by lyric basses)

Edgar	Puccini	Father	one aria
Faust	Gounod	Valentin	"Avant de quitter"
Falstaff	Verdi	Ford	Monologue
Le Nozze di Figaro	Mozart	Count	"Hai già vinta la causa"
Pagliacci	Leoncavallo	Silvio	duet with Nedda
Tannhäuser	Wagner	Wolfram	two arias
La Traviata	Verdi	Germont	"Di Provenza"
Der Wildschütz	Lortzing	Count	one aria
Zar und Zimmerman	Lortzing	Czar	"Mit Krone und Szepter"
Die Zauberflöte	Mozart	Papageno	three arias

DRAMATIC BARITONE/BASS BARITONE

Aïda	Verdi	Amonasro	"Ma tu Re"
Andrea Chenier	Giordano	Gerard	two arias
Un Ballo in Maschera	Verdi	Renato	two arias
Carmen	Bizet	Escamillo	"Votre Toast"
Cavalleria Rusticana	Mascagni	Alfio	"Il cavallo scalpita"
Les Contes d'Hoffmann	Offenbach	Dappertutto/Lindorf	two arias
Don Carlos	Verdi	Rodrigo (Posa)	two arias
Falstaff	Verdi	Falstaff	two arias
Guillaume Tell	Rossini	Tell	"Sois immobile"

(Frequently sung as "Resta immobile" from Italian version.)

Otello	Verdi	Iago	"Era la notte"/"Credo"
Pagliacci	Leoncavallo	Tonio	"Si puo! (Prologo)"
Rigoletto	Verdi	Rigoletto	"Pari siamo"/"Cortigiani"
Il tabarro	Puccini	Michele	"Nulla silenzio"
Tosca	Puccini	Scarpia	"Te Deum"
Il Trovatore	Verdi	Conte di Luna	"Il balen"

HELDEN BARITONE/ DRAMATIC BASS

Boris Godunov	Mussorgsky	Boris	three arias
Boris Godunov	Mussorgsky	Varlaam	"Kazan Aria"
Don Carlos	Verdi	Phillip	"Ella giammai m'amo"
Elektra	R. Strauss	Oreste	no aria
Fidelio	Beethoven	Don Pizarro	"Ha! welch ein Augenblick"
Der Fliegende Holländer	Wagner	Dutchman	"Die Frist ist um"
Lohengrin	Wagner	Telramund	one aria
Die lustigen Weiber von Windsor	Nicolai	Falstaff	one aria
Meistersinger von Nürnberg	Wagner	Hans Sachs	two arias
Parsifal	Wagner	Amfortas	two arias
Parsifal	Wagner	Gurnemanz	Act 1 Narrative/ Good Friday Spell
Ring Cycle	Wagner		
Das Rheingold		Wotan	Entry into Valhalla
Das Rheingold		Alberich	Curse
Die Walküre		Wotan	Farewell
Salome	R. Strauss	Jochanaan	"Er ist in einem Nache"
Susannah	Floyd	Olin Blitch	two arias

BASS (BUFFO/SERIOSO)

Il barbiere di Siviglia	Rossini	Basilio	"La calunnia"
Il barbiere di Siviglia	Rossini	Bartolo	"Ho un dottor"
The Bartered Bride	Smetana	Kecal	one aria
La Bohème	Puccini	Colline	"Vecchia zimarra"
Cenerentola	Rossini	Magnifico	one aria

Opera	Composer	Character	Arias
Cenerentola	Rossini	Alidoro	three arias
Don Giovanni	Mozart	Leporello	two arias
Don Giovanni	Mozart	Masetto	"Ho capito"
Entführung aus dem Serail	Mozart	Osmin	three arias
Faust	Gounod	Mephistopheles	two arias
Fidelio	Beethoven	Rocco	"Das Gold"
Der Fliegende Holländer	Wagner	Daland	one aria
Der Freischütz	Weber	Kaspar	two arias
Lohengrin	Wagner	König Heinrich	one aria
Mefistofele	Boito	Mefistofele	"Il Mondo"
Nabucco	Verdi	Zaccaria	one aria
Le Nozze di Figaro	Mozart	Figaro	three arias
Le Nozze di Figaro	Mozart	Bartolo	one aria
Les Vêspres Siciliennes	Verdi	Procida	"O toi Palerme"
Der Wildschütz	Lortzing	Bacculus	one aria
Yevghenyi Onegin	Tchaikovsky	Gremin	one aria
Die Zauberflöte	Mozart	Sarastro	two arias

From the above list, arias from *Don Carlos* and *Les Vêspres Siciliennes* may be sung in either Italian or French. French is the original, but until recently this was seldom used and is still not the norm. Either is acceptable. Original keys and languages are usually required by competitions, but traditional transpositions from *Il Barbiere di Siviglia* for Rosina and Basilio arias are so frequently used that they too may be acceptable. Transpositions of certain arias should not be used because the point of singing the aria, other than being artistic, is to prove that the singer has those difficult high notes! I have not listed too many unusual-language operas here because they are only occasionally given in the West. I have not listed every role in each opera mentioned, nor have I listed every aria for each character. Some roles have extra arias but one main one. Some operas listed are not frequent visitors to Western theaters, but in the interest of the coach being advisor, these are listed as possible roles to be encountered in Europe.

APPENDIX B

NOTABLE AND RECOMMENDED EDITIONS

THE CRITERIA FOR THE FOLLOWING discussion of the best editions to use need to be explained. Any score printed, piano-vocal or orchestral, should be complete — all music should be there. Traditional cuts may or may not be indicated, but no edition is really very good that omits music, no matter how typical the cut may be. Consequently, I cannot recommend the G. Schirmer *Lucia di Lammermoor* or *Le Nozze di Figaro*. The *Lucia* has a major omission of coda material at the end of the Enrico-Lucia duet. In *Figaro*, they omit part of the "Aprite, presto, aprite" duettino. These are both now performed complete quite regularly and need to be printed.

Some scores will be coming out soon in critical editions that will restore much of the omitted music, sometimes including music that has not been heard in years. At least such restorations allow the production teams to know what was really written and can be performed.

In *Lucia* the question of keys also arises. I will discuss this more below. *Figaro* contains two versions of certain passages — notably the second-act trio for Susanna, the Countess, and the Count. Both versions should be printed in any edition that is to be considered really good. Schirmer prints only the revised version, and Bärenreiter prints only the original. Thus neither gets it right.

All music must be correct down to the last dotted note. This is very difficult to edit, but that's the point of critical editions. Consequently, the Bärenreiter *Figaro* is preferable, mainly because it gets all of the rhythms correct (the exception being the curious mistake on the word "garofani" mentioned in the chapter about Mozart).

It would be helpful if an edition printed really standard transpositions in the piano-vocal scores, and indicated "if a transposition of the following aria is made, the transposition begins here" and how it is done. This is true for *Il Barbiere di Siviglia* and for *La Bohème*. Orchestral material frequently comes printed in two keys.

Study of manuscripts/autographs can reveal just how difficult editing can be. Some composers are quite clean and clear — for example, Mozart is quite easy to read. But other composers scratch out and use such shortcuts that the chance of knowing exactly what they ultimately wanted is purely speculation (see Bellini's autograph for *Norma*). In some cases it can be necessary to use more than one score as reference.

BAROQUE OPERAS

Handel: Bärenreiter now prints the clearest edition of these works. They have most if not all of Handel's works in print. The older Chrysander edition has virtues not to be totally ignored, but the scholarship just isn't quite as complete as it might be. Still, in works like *Alcina*, the older edition gives indications of music that does not and should appear in the Bärenreiter printing, including different keys for some arias. Handel may have rewritten *Alcina*, but some conductors prefer the original version. His *Messiah* is available in a very good and inexpensive edition from Oxford University Press. This includes all of the alternatives!

Scarlatti: Few will need to search for Scarlatti scores, but Harvard University Press once had a complete edition of his important scores. They are not all still available, but they were complete and scholarly, with alternate versions and changes placed in the appendix.

Vivaldi: I haven't seen a publisher for his operas yet, possibly because I have yet to coach one of them. Cecilia Bartoli's recent championing of his operas may change that situation.

MOZART

Surprisingly, Dover Editions are very clear and mostly excellent orchestral scores. They come from the Peters Editions, Georg Schünemann and Kurt Soldan, editors. More recent scholarship points to the Neue Mozart Ausgabe for both orchestral scores and piano-vocal scores. These are printed by Bärenreiter. The piano reductions are very good and contain more correct markings than any other scores. In the case of works like *Idomeneo*, all music is printed and all options for each role (Idamante in that opera is printed both as tenor and as mezzo-soprano). In such discussions, it may seem strange to carp, but Bärenreiter could put more music on a page and save the coach so many page turns. Although it may seem silly, in a work like *Idomeneo* or *Figaro* it makes a large difference. Undoubtedly, G. Schirmer has the most frequently sung translations, though Andrew Porter's excellent translations are now printed in some editions based on the NMA. Unfortunately, the G. Schirmer *Die Zauberflöte* prints only a cut version of the dialogue, making it impossible to include more if desired, and more complete dialogue is becoming the norm. (The uncut dialogue is very interesting to read, but it is quite difficult to get an international cast to speak it well.)

Any coach should keep on top of trends of thought. In that way, they can understand the reasons behind the occasional desire to rearrange act 3 of *Le Nozze di Figaro* or whether to have a mezzo-soprano or tenor singing Idamante in *Idomeneo*.

BEL CANTO OPERAS

Dover Edition orchestral scores are generally available and are not bad, though they are not the best Dover prints. For orchestral scores and parts, Ricordi should be followed.

Rossini: The new Fondazione Rossini editions are recommended above all others. These are published in piano-vocal score by Ricordi. The orchestral scores are becoming more available, too. Not all of the operas are available as yet, but the editing process continues through each opera. So far *Guillaume Tell, La Cenerentola, Otello, Il Barbiere di Siviglia, Ermione,* and others exist. Other than critical editions, Ricordi is still preferable to others for Rossini's operas. In some scores, such as *Il Cambiale di Matrimonio,* the errors are many and obvious to the discerning eye.

Bellini: Other than *Norma,* most scores of Bellini are fairly straightforward and have fewer alterations. I believe Ricordi is embarking on these operas in critical editions, too. It is to be hoped so. *Norma,* particularly, exists in various editions, with orchestral scores seldom agreeing with piano-vocal scores. In some places even the manuscript is a quagmire of cuts, rewrites, and the like. "Casta diva" appears variously in F or G (the original and more difficult), and other changes affect not only exact notes to be sung but also how long certain movements are.

The soft ending to the "Guerra" chorus in fact involves some editorial working by the conductor.

La Sonnambula appears almost universally in transposed keys, since the keys for the original tenor part (written for Rubini) are out of reach for most tenors, even those who specialize in that repertoire. Perhaps a critical edition will restore exactly what Bellini wrote and then print the transpositions as well.

Donizetti: Critical editions are emerging quickly of his works as well. Again the publisher is Ricordi. Even the "non-critical" editions are now respectable. But *Lucia di Lammermoor* and *L'Elisir d'amore* were in need of clean, new editions, and Casa Ricordi has provided these. Although G. Schirmer piano-vocal scores of these works are more accessible, *L'Elisir* in particular has some notable problems in the editing process wherein spurious phrase markings confuse singers and coaches alike. The Ricordi *Don Pasquale* also has one of the best printed translations ever of any opera.

BEETHOVEN AND WEBER AND NICOLAI

I tend to favor Boosey & Hawkes for Beethoven's *Fidelio*, but that is possibly because I like the reduction. It sounds more complete somehow than G. Schirmer. Weber operas are not usually performed, but the Dover orchestral score of *Der Freischütz* is quite good, including all of the dialogue, even the brief scene frequently omitted at the beginning of act 3. Since this is a reprint of the Peters Edition, one can be sure that the Peters piano-vocal score is also worthy of consideration. G. Schirmer has some minor errors in *Der Freischütz*, though it includes a listing of what instrument plays each number (always helpful). The printing, however, makes many rhythms quite difficult to read, due to even printing of uneven rhythms.

For Otto Nicolai's *Die Lustigen Weiber von Windsor*, I suggest Peters again. If someone wishes to perform the work in English, then the piano-vocal score of G. Schirmer is fine, since it uses the same musical plates as the Peters. G. Schirmer, unfortunately, makes some cuts and includes only English, precluding use of German language for study of arias, duets, or dialogue.

HUMPERDINCK

While we're on Germanic opera, Humperdinck's *Hänsel und Gretel* is best again in the Peters edition. That is true for two reasons. Peters is in German only and also there are certain rhythms in the final waltz inaccurately printed in the more generally available G. Schirmer. Otherwise, Schirmer is quite good, with a very playable reduction, which retains most of the cues needed. Both nicely isolate the cuckoo line so an offstage conductor can use the piano-vocal score instead of a full score for cues to the cuckoo and echo voices. The Dover orchestral score is quite good, too.

VERDI

After years of inadequate piano-vocal scores and orchestral parts for Verdi operas, Ricordi is finally rectifying this problem by extending their critical scores to Verdi's entire oeuvre. This has involved a great deal of work to uncover long-lost sections of music and earlier versions of scenes now performed in recomposed variants. Most notable in the new editions is the score for *Don Carlos*, published in French, Italian, and German (but not English!) singing texts. It tries to put forth every variant that Verdi wrote for the opera, and includes the huge ballet as well. Other operas have been appearing, as has the *Requiem*. Some critical editions, such as *Falstaff*, are hampered by the difficulty in finding orchestral originals, even when piano-vocal scores exist. But the mainstream operas like *Rigoletto* and *Don Carlos* are readily available in piano-vocal scores and full scores.

FRENCH OPERAS

The existence of critical editions in French operas is in a woeful state. Although the works of Hector Berlioz have appeared in new and wonderfully complete editions, the works of Charles Gounod, Georges Bizet, and Jules Massenet have not. Even the later composers, like Saint-Säens, Debussy, and Fauré, could use more care.

Gounod: *Faust* had so many alterations made to it during the rehearsal process that one can hardly have any idea what Gounod wanted in some places. The autograph exists and should be made the basis for a completely thorough restudy of the music. In the absence of that, Fritz Oeser, whose editions are questionable in other ways, here has the best possible edition, since all he did was take all previous editions and combine the most accurate readings of each section. He did not, however, have access to those sections that appear only in the autograph. Where are Faust's cabaletta (with the only sung mention of his name!), Marguerite's mad scene, the little scene with the girls offstage, and numerous smaller sections? The autograph could open a few eyes at the portions it shows that have never been heard, but so much remains lost. *Roméo et Juliette* is a much easier problem, yet there is no completely accurate score there either. The G. Schirmer, a reprint of the revised piano-vocal score, gives all scenes complete — in a sense. Only the ballet music and a chorus in the wedding are missing. But the orchestral material does not include some of that music. It will come as quite a surprise to a coach or a singer to find whole sections missing from particularly act 1. The original piano-vocal score shows even more startling music, particularly in act 3. Unlike *Faust*, where inclusion of omitted music might mean another forty-five minutes, the "lost" music in *Roméo et Juliette* would probably amount to no more than fifteen minutes. In addition to the "complete" music recorded in the most recent EMI recording, these are the complete coda to the first scene, an aria for Frère Laurent with offstage chorus at the beginning of the wedding scene, a central section to the wedding scene, and an extension to the fight scene (actually an alternate version of the scene, though portions could be taken to strengthen the scene even more). Oddly enough, the difficulty of making this material available is minimal, since many older orchestral parts include the music crudely crossed out. Editions Choudens seems to show no interest in rectifying this matter.

BIZET

Carmen exists, of course, in the much-maligned Oeser edition. It has many failings, but also some important variants not printed elsewhere. A better critical edition has not appeared. Oeser's most flagrant excesses are reversion to earlier readings of certain melodic cells that were changed for the better before the composer died — and since he died only months after *Carmen's* premiere, that is saying something. Oeser also reverts to an early reading of Escamillo's exit in act 3 scene 1, and to a spurious outburst at the killing of Carmen (although it is quite exciting!).

Les Pêcheurs des Perles has been edited and reissued with many excisions and alterations restored. These affect many moments, but most notably the end of the famous duet for the tenor and baritone and also the duet for the soprano and baritone. Always investigate the publishing date and seek the most recent. There are not many editions of this opera from which to choose.

MASSENET

G. Schirmer actually has a good edition for *Manon*. International Edition prints a good *Werther* (apparently only one translation and printing of that opera exists, and International makes the French edition available most easily). His other operas are not frequently given. For orchestral scores, turn to Edition Choudens, although Dover's *Manon* has some interesting variants in a place or two. (A good critical edition of both would be a blessing.)

DEBUSSY

Pélleas et Mélisande is a wonderful opera, but there are discrepancies between scores that affect rhythms, scoring, and barring. The Dover orchestral score is an earlier version of the score, and certain rebarrings took place in the revision. I believe that there is a critical edition of this score that includes a portion of the Yniold/Golaud scene cut before the premiere and frequently reinstated today. Seek it out. For a traditional view, International is readily available, and it is mostly accurate.

OFFENBACH

Les Contes d'Hoffmann has been a particularly open field of contention for years. What did Offenbach really intend? Oeser's edition, published, as are all his editions, by Editions Alkor, printed by Bärenreiter, is filled with honest attempts to fill out the portions left incomplete by Offenbach. The problem is that many, many pages of music have been discovered in the years since that edition emerged. Now the edition to study — unfortunately rental only (so I understand) — is the Michael Kaye edition. Various recordings of both his grand opera (recitative) and opéra comique (dialogue) editions have been issued. The problem for the opera in general is that there is too much of a good thing. In one place Offenbach wrote three, interchangeable arias for Giulietta! What to do? In the operettas the problems are now becoming less. While Belwin Mills once started an aborted edition of the complete Offenbach (mostly unavailable now), Boosey & Hawkes is now issuing Offenbach Edition Keck (OEK), with critical answers to the various problems and variants between performing versions. It is to be hoped that this edition reaches completion and remains available to us for a long time. While I've only seen the orchestral score and piano-vocal score for *Orphée aux Enfers*, it promises to be an excellent answer to the problems encountered in earlier editions. An example of these problems can be found in *La Périchole*. The "Met" version includes music from other sources, transpositions, and a shortened dialogue (not printed with the music!) that obscures some important facts and niceties of the original dialogue. It would be wonderful if Boosey &

Hawkes (also publisher of the "Met" version) would put new English translations in these new scores. The *Orphée* had only French and German. Many companies that perform operas in the original languages revert to English for operettas. An English translation included in the CD-ROM that accompanied the orchestral score only is not a good answer.

WAGNER

The music dramas of Wagner have also been undergoing a thorough cleansing and editing. Perhaps most interesting of these for a scholar would be the earliest operas: *Das Liebesverbot, Die Feen*, and *Rienzi, der letze Tribun.* Though those are not performed much, all of the operas are being scoured for mistakes. These are not as prevalent in the later operas, but in *Dutchman, Tannhäuser,* and *Lohengrin* the problems can still be quite a trial. G. Schirmer vocal scores are not bad, except in *Tannhäuser,* where the multiplicity of editions confounds them. For that opera, I'd suggest the Peters Edition. Many of the published piano vocal scores use the same printing plates but interchange translations.

RICHARD STRAUSS

Richard Strauss's operas may pose many problems, but printed editions are not among them. Until most recently Boosey & Hawkes in America (Fürstner Verlag in Europe) has been the exclusive publisher. So if mistakes exist, they can only be rectified by careful study, not by changing editions. Those now emerging from copyright are still printed in the plates from Boosey and Hawkes.

PUCCINI

Ricordi is bringing out critical editions of Puccini's operas, too, uncovering many minor details even in operas as well known as *La Bohème. Turandot* may even emerge with more than one ending — take your pick! *La Fanciulla del West* has a small section in act 1 that was only recorded for the first time by Eva Marton, Ben Heppner, and Leonard Slatkin.

More recent works of Berg, Britten, and others are generally available in only one edition, and since these are the original publishers one must hope they are accurate, though Ricordi's earlier editions show that such an assumption could be a major mistake.

APPENDIX C

FAVORITE CATCH PHRASES

I HOPE NO ONE WILL take these as merely funny things to say. True, they have a certain levity, but a very important purpose lurks behind each one of them.

1. I understand every word you said — but you don't! This means that the singer is singing quite accurately and clearly each syllable, vowel, and consonant. But the meaning is not coming through. Hence the idea that I can understand the "verbal diction" but not the "thought diction."
2. "Thought diction" means literally the projection of the meaning of the word beyond the presence of vowels, consonants, and syllables. This can involve projecting the active part of words — "uscite dal mio petto" from Susanna's recitative before "Deh vieni non tardar" (in *Le Nozze di Figaro*) should have a certain mild force to it, "banishing" the very cares from her heart. It can also mean simply connecting with the meaning of the text. When Butterfly's "Un bel di vedremo" becomes a narrative and not an aria, then the singer is projecting her "thought diction."
3. "Optimum roar range." This is that portion of a singer's voice in which he or she can produce the most sound, at times too much sound to balance. It is usually used in conjunction with trying to balance an ensemble where one voice is quite high and another is quite low. In the entrance music at the beginning of act 3 of *Carmen*, Don José is written quite high, very much in

his optimum roar range. Unfortunately, this means he will have major difficulties in balancing the rest of the ensemble. The bottom of a voice is not usually considered a roar range at all, but between the first and second *passaggi* can be quite loud and difficult to control.

4. The words are "Tra-la-la-la," not "Tra-lol-lol-lol." I discovered this problem working on the first scene of *Hänsel und Gretel*. Singers have a major tendency to sing "lol" instead of "la" — particularly when the syllables follow in close proximity, as there. The problem with that is that it causes almost immediate tension in the tongue, down in the throat. "La" is both easier and causes no tension, but it is a chore to get the singers to stop old habits.

5. "Mut-tair, Fah-tair." Young singers are not the only ones to make this mistake. "Mutter" and "Vater" in German are pronounced much more closely to the English way than the fashion shown in the heading. But, because "der" is pronounced so closely to "dare" in the English language — even more properly, one might say "day-uh" — the singer assumes that the "-er" in the unaccented syllables of those two words and many others should be pronounced in the same fashion. This is inaccurate, of course, but it persists. Knowledge of the International Phonetic Alphabet (IPA) will help a singer learn more accurately the differences in languages. Coaches would do well to learn it, too, in order to teach more effectively.

6. "Three vibrati on the unaccented syllable" syndrome. This happens particularly in Italian literature, recitative, and arioso. But it is not exclusive to that language and literature at all. What is it? Take Cherubino's "Non so più..." The first line ends with the word "faccio." The accent falls on the first syllable, but countless singers, wanting just a little more "tone" to come through, allow the second syllable, "-cio," to elongate to almost twice its length. In recitative this causes words to become improperly stressed and actually bad Italian. It is not something exclusive to young singers either. I once heard a good Leporello sing, "Madaminaaaaa, il catologo e questoooooo..." You get the point. The remedy is to stress the proper syllable, in recitatives making it a hair longer, and tapering off of the wrong note quickly. It takes practice and perseverence from coach and singer alike.

7. No arias not written by the composer. This refers, again in recitative, to the way some singers, particularly students, start singing the recitatives with too much legato, notably on certain short

phrases. It does not refer to the practice of more legato singing at the end of a recitative.

8. I didn't know your name was Rossini! The last word would also be Mozart, Beethoven, Wagner, or whomever. It refers to the singer's ability to invent rhythms and notes, not following the composer's written instructions. An example might be Laetitia's recitative and aria from Menotti's *Old Maid and the Thief*: "Steal me, oh, steal me, sweet thief." I cannot say how many people treat the rhythms in the recitative casually, as if Menotti had no idea exactly what he wanted. If he writes a triplet on the words, "The old woman sighs...," he means a triplet, not an eighth and two sixteenths. Similar mistakes happen all through the recitative. American singers seem to think that if it's in English, no one will notice the inventive, rhythmic "improvements." In Rossini it happens in passagework and does not refer to purposeful alterations of the passages for embellishment. It means they learned the passage wrong, a problem for singers of all composers.

9. You just slipped into another language! This actually refers to those moments when a singer mispronounces a word in one language as if it were part of another language. The usual mistake is "qui" being pronounced as "chi" — I accuse the singer of coming directly from singing in French. It can happen in other languages, however, and it is one of the dangers of learning to sing intelligibly in more than one language.

10. "But it's not that way on the recording." This says a lot more than the singer saying it thinks it does. It seems to say that the recording is correct and the coach is wrong. Both are fallible, but most important is that there is more than "the" recording to consider. How many recordings has the singer listened to? "The" would indicate only one. When a singer says that, I answer with, "Which is 'the' recording? Who is on it? Who conducts?" The student frequently can't answer these questions. Today, few singers know about the tendency of certain conductors to be notably slow (Karajan) or fast (Böhm) in their late years.

These are the primary phrases I have used or with which I have had to deal. They are examples of phrases that can be used to make a point but still keep the coaching light and in a good working mood.

NOTES

Preface

1. Quoted from a guest lecture given by Virgil Thomson at Indiana University, which the author heard during the mid-1970s. It is also discussed in Thomson's book *Music with Words, a Composer's View* (New Haven and London: Yale University Press, 1959), pp. 60–61.

Chapter 1

1. Three examples of valuable books on diction are *Singing in French: A Manual of French Diction and French Vocal Repertoire* by Thomas Grubb; *A Handbook of Diction for Singers: Italian, German, French* by David Adams; and *The Singer's Manual of English Diction* by Madeleine Marshall. Even English needs some study and care.
2. Helena Matheopoulos, *Placido Domingo, My Operatic Roles* (New York: Little, Brown and Company, 2000), p. 18.
3. In Gounod's opera *Faust*, the farewell duet between Valentin and Marguerite, cut before the premiere but available on at least one recording, begins with exactly the same figuration as the Beethoven sonata. It is even in the same key, and is scored for horns. One must wonder if Gounod is making a veiled reference to the Beethoven work, also a "Farewell."
4. G. Ricordi & C. Editori — Milano, Luigi Ricci, *Variazioni — Cadenze — Tradizioni per Canto*, Vol. 1 (*Voci femminili* — 1937, *Voci maschili* — 1937, *Voci miste* — 1939, *Variazioni e cadenze per G. Rossini* — 1941).
5. G. Schirmer — New York 1943, *The Estelle Liebling book of Coloratura Cadenzas: Containing Traditional and New Cadenzas, Cuts, Technical Exercises, and Suggested Concert Programs*, compiled, arranged, and edited by Estelle Liebling. The famous coloratura soprano Beverly Sills was a student of Estelle Liebling.
6. The dramatic similarities between these two arias is remarkable, but they also have other musical similarities. For example, in *La Traviata*, the "Gypsy Chorus" in the party scene at Flora's house is in E minor, evoking the primary key for Azucena in *Il Trovatore*.
7. Richard Miller, *The Structure of Singing: System and Art in Vocal Technique* (New York: Schirmer Books; London: Collier Macmillan, 1986).

Chapter 2

1. Handel would sometimes delay the writing of the secco recitatives until quite late in the compositional process. He would tell the singers to rehearse the passages as dialogue, with natural inflections and pacing, so they would have few problems adding the notes when he had written them down.

Interlude 1

1. *Webster's New World Dictionary of the American Language: College Edition* (Cleveland and New York: The World Publishing Company, 1962).

Chapter 3

1. The late Tibor Kozma was for many years a teacher of conducting at Indiana University. Before that he had conducted at the Metropolitan Opera and many orchestras throughout the United States and Europe. Most people said that he hated recordings, but he would always correct such people by saying, "That is not so. Recordings are fine before or after — but not instead of." He then would proceed to fill out his proverb by explaining that he meant "before study or after study of a score, but not instead of study of a score." Even in the 1960s singers were already learning their roles through recordings.
2. Daniel Majeske, former concertmaster of the Cleveland Orchestra, stated shortly before he died that the volume of orchestras all over the world had risen by many decibels in the time he had been with the Cleveland Orchestra.

Chapter 4

1. In Britain, the director is often called the producer. In the United States, the producer mostly deals with the uppermost administrative details of the production and oversees the budget.
2. Ionazzi, Daniel A. *The Stage Management Handbook*. (Cincinnati, Ohio: Betterway Books, 1992).
3. Clark, Mark Ross *Singing, Acting, and Movement in Opera: A guide to Singer-getics*. (Bloomington, Indiana: Indiana University Press, 2002).

Chapter 8

1. *Great Shakespeareans*, Pearl GEMM CD 9465 (Pavilion Records Ltd, Sparrows Green, Wadhurst, E. Sussex, England). This is a recording of great actors of the past, including Lewis Waller, John Gielgud, Edwin Booth, Arthur Bourchier, Ben Greet, John Barrymore, Henry Ainsley, Sir Herbert Beerbohm Tree, and Maurice Evans.
2. Michael Leverson Meyer, *Ibsen: A Biography* (Garden City, New York: Doubleday & Company, Inc.), pp. 70–71.

3. I am reminded of a demonstration given once on *The Wonderful World of Disney*. Two dozen or so mousetraps were set up on a table with Ping-Pong balls resting on them. Then one Ping-Pong ball was thrown. The reaction that one ball got from the two dozen or so mousetraps/Ping-Pong balls was impressive and immediate.
4. Hans Busch, trans. and ed., *Verdi's Aïda: The History of an Opera in Letters and Documents* (Minneapolis: University of Minnesota Press, 1978).

Chapter 9

1. *My Fair Lady* by Alan Jay Lerner and Frederick Loewe, copyright 1956 by Coward-McCann, New York.

ANNOTATED BIBLIOGRAPHY

Appendix B listed a variety of desirable scores and why they are desirable. The following annotated bibliography deals with sources I have used in the preparation of this text and some that should be valuable to anyone entering the profession of opera coach.

Adams, David. A Handbook of Diction for Singers: Italian, German, French. *New York: Oxford University Press, 1999. This book offers some of the best and most comprehensive rules on good diction in the three major operatic languages.*

Busch, Hans, trans. and ed. Verdi's Aïda. The History of an Opera in Letters and Documents. *Minneapolis: University of Minnesota Press, 1978. Reading the letters and the* Disposizione scenica *of such an important opera might seem dull to some, but this book reads easily and shows us not only the composer but also the opinions he held on many singers of his time.*

Castel, Nico. French Opera Libretti/with International Phonetic Alphabet transcriptions, word for word translations, including a guide to the I.P.A. and notes on the French transcriptions. *Edited by Scott Jackson Wiley. Geneseo, N.Y.: Leyerle, 1999–2000. This series of rather expensive books saves hours with dictionaries and heavy study. Not only does the I.P.A. help every singer and coach, but the translations and footnotes are also invaluable and perceptive. They are a must for most coaches. Vol. 1. Werther; Carmen; Samson et Dalila; Lakmé; Pelléas et Mélisande; Chérubin; Don Carlos (French version); Les Contes d'Hoffmann. Vol. 2. Faust; Roméo et Juliette; La Juive; Mignon; Hamlet; Thaïs; Les pêcheurs de perles; Manon.*

———. Italian Belcanto Opera Libretti/with International Phonetic Alphabet transcriptions and word for word translations, including a guide to the I.P.A. and notes on Italian phonetics. *Edited by Scott Jackson Wiley. Geneseo, N. Leyerle, 2000–2002. Vol. 1.* Il barbiere di Siviglia *(Rossini);* Il turco in Italia *(Rossini);* Lucia di Lammermoor *(Donizetti);* Norma *(Bellini);* I Capuleti e I Montecchi *(Bellini). Vol. 2.* La Cenerentola *(Rossini);* L'italiana in Algeri *(Rossini);* La sonnambula *(Bellini);* Anna Bolena *(Donizetti);* Maria Stuarda *(Donizetti);* Roberto Devereux *(Donizetti);* Don Pasquale *(Donizetti);* I Puritani *(Bellini). Vol. 3.* Guillaume Tell *(Rossini);* Le Comte Ory *(Rossini);* Otello *(Rossini);* Semiramide *(Rossini);* La fille du regiment *(Donizetti);* La favorite *(Donizetti);* Beatrice di Tenda *(Bellini).*

———. Italian verismo opera libretti/with International Phonetic Alphabet transcriptions and word for word translations, including a guide to the I.P.A. and notes in Italian phonetics. *Edited by Scott Jackson Wiley. Geneseo, N.Y.: Leyerle, 2000. Vol. 1.* Andrea Chénier *(Giordano);* Fedora *(Giordano);* Adriana Lecouvreur *(Cilea);* La Bohème *(Leoncavallo);* Mefistofele *(Boito);* Cavalleria Rusticana *(Mascagni);* I Pagliacci *(Leoncavallo);* La Gioconda *(Ponchielli);* L'Amico Fritz *(Mascagni) (Vol. 2 is not yet available.)*

———. The libretti of Mozart's completed operas/in two volumes with International Phonetic Alphabet transcriptions, word for word translations, including a guide to the I.P.A. and notes on the Italian and German transcriptions by Nico Castel. *Foreword by Julius Rudel; Illustrations by Eugene Green. Geneseo, N. Leyerle, 1997–1998. Vol. 1.* Bastien und Bastienne; La Clemenza di Tito; Cosi fan tutte; Don Giovanni; Die Entführung aus dem Serail; La finta giardiniera; La finta semplice. *Vol. 2.* Idomeneo, Lucio Silla; Mitridate, re di Ponto; Le nozze di Figaro; Il re pastore; Der Schauspieldirektor; Die Zauberflöte.

———. The complete Puccini libretti/with International Phonetic Alphabet transcriptions, word for word translations, including a guide to the I.P.A. and notes on the Italian transcriptions by Nico Castel. *Foreword by Sherrill Milnes; Illustrations by Eugene Green. Edited by Marcie Stapp. Geneseo, N. Leyerle, 2002. Vol. 1.* La Bohème; Edgar; La Fanciulla del West; Madama Butterfly; Manon Lescaut. *Vol. 2.* La Rondine; Tosca; Il Trittico: Il Tabarro, Suor Angelica, Gianni Schicchi; Le Villi.

———. Four Strauss opera libretti/with International Phonetic Alphabet transcriptions, word for word translations, including a guide to the German I.P.A. and notes on the German transcriptions by Nico Castel. *Edited by Marcie Stapp; foreword by Evelyn Lear. Geneseo, N. Leyerle, 2002.* Der Rosenkavalier, Elektra, Salome, Ariadne auf Naxos.

———. The complete Verdi libretti/ with International Phonetic Alphabet transcriptions, word for word translations, including a guide to the I.P.A. and notes on the Italian transcriptions by Nico Castel. *Foreword by Sherrill Milnes; illustrations by Eugene Green. Geneseo, N. Leyerele,*

1994–1996. Vol. 1. Aïda, Alzira; Aroldo; Attila; Un Ballo in maschera; La Battaglia di Legnano; Il Corsaro. *Vol. 2.* Don Carlo; I due Foscari; Ernani; Falstaff; La Forza del Destino; Un Giorno di Regno; Giovanna D'Arco. *Vol. 3.* I Lombardi; Luisa Miller; Macbeth; I Masnadieri; Nabucco; Oberto; Otello. *Vol. 4.* Rigoletto; Simon Boccanegra; Stiffelio; La traviata; Il Trovatore; I Vespri Siciliani.

Clark, Mark Ross. Singing, Acting and Movement in Opera: A Guide to Singer-getics. *Bloomington: Indiana University Press, 2002.*

Goldovsky, Boris and Schoep, Arthur. Bringing Soprano Arias to Life. *Drawings by Leo Van Witsen. New York: G. Schirmer, 1973. Good ideas about various standard repertoire arias.*

Grubb, Thomas. Singing in French: A Manual of French Diction and French Vocal Repertoire. *Foreword by Pierre Bernac. New York: Schirmer Books, 1979.*

Ionazzi, Daniel A. The Stage Management Handbook. *Cincinnati: Betterway Books, 1992.*

Lerner, Alan Jay and Loewe, Frederick. My Fair Lady. *New York: Coward-McCann, 1956.*

Liebling, Estelle, comp. and ed. The Estelle Liebling Book of Coloratura Cadenzas: Containing Traditional and New Cadenzas, Cuts, Technical Exercises, and Suggested Concert Programs. *New York: G. Schirmer, 1943.*

Marshall, Madeleine. The Singer's Manual of English Diction. *New York: G. Schirmer, 1953. One of the first books to codify the pronunciation of the English language for singers.*

Matheopoulos, Helena. Placido Domingo: My Operatic Roles. *New York: Little, Brown and Company, 2000.*

Meyer, Michael Leverson. Ibsen: A Biography. *Garden City, N.Y.: Doubleday & Company, Inc., 1971.*

Miller, Richard. On the Art of Singing. *New York: Oxford University Press, 1996. Any coach can gain much more vocal understanding from studying this book and the next, which are well written and very clear.*

———. The Structure of Singing: System and Art in Vocal Technique. *New York: Schirmer Books, 1986.*

Northrop, Henry Davenport. The Delsarte Speaker of Modern Elocution: Student edition. *Compiled and edited by Henry Davenport Northrop. [Entered according to Act of Congress, in the year 1895, by J. R. Jones, to the Office of the Librarian of Congress, at Washington, D.C.]*

Ricci, Luigi. Variazioni — Cadenze — Tradizioni per Canto. *Milan: G. Ricordi & C. Edition. Vol. 1. — Voci femminili — c. 1937. Vol. 2. — Voci maschili — c. 1939. Vol. 3. — Voci miste — c. 1939. Vol. 4. — Variazioni e cadenze per Rossini — c. 1941.*

Rickards, Steven. 20th Century Countertenor Repertoire. *Lanham, Md.: Scarecrow Press, 2006. A listing of music written since 1900 specifically for countertenor.*

Singher, Martial. An Interpretive Guide to Operatic Arias: A Handbook for Singers, Coaches, Teachers, and Students. *Translations of the texts of the arias by Eta and Martial Singher. University Park: Pennsylvania State University Press, 1983. Similar to Goldovsky's volume, this deals with arias in all voice categories. It gives good ideas to consider about vocal and dramatic needs of the aria.*

Thomson, Virgil. Music with Words, a Composer's View. *New Haven and London: Yale University Press, 1959.*

Webster's New World Dictionary of the American Language: College Edition. Cleveland and New York: *The World Publishing Company, 1962.*

DISCOGRAPHY:

Great Shakespeareans. *Pearl GEMM CD 9465. Sparrows Green, Wadhurst, E. Sussex, England: Pavilion Records, Ltd. Compact disc. This compact disc is a fascinating compilation of monologues from some of the early twentieth century's greatest actors. It shows the incredible changes in acting in the works of even so seminal an author as Shakespeare.*

INDEX

A

Accent, errors in, 7, 119, 147
Accidentals, 4
Accompanists, 55, 61–63
Adagio, 118, 119
Adamo, Mark, 168
Adams, John, 81, 128, 162, 164
Adrianna Lecouvreur, 156
Aïda, 118–119, 128
Alagna, 13
Albert Herring, 163, 167
Alcina, 85, 87, 98
Allegro vivace, 102
Amahl and the Night Visitors, 163
Amelia al Ballo, 163
Ancora più vivo, 40
Andanta, 118
Andantino, 118
Andrea Chenier, 27, 155
Andrés, Don, 25
Appoggiaturas, 27–28, 94
Argento, Dominick, 162
Ariadne auf Naxos, 61
Arioso, 82
Assistant director, 43
Assistant stage manager (ASM), 42
Auditioning, 55–69
Audition notebook, preparing, 56

B

Bach, 90
Ballet, 131
Banda interna, 53, 120
Barber, Samuel, 11
Barbier, Jules, 131
Bar form, 152
Baroque era, 4, 21, 34, 81–90
The Bartered Bride, 10, 27
Bastien und Bastienne, 91
Battistini, Mattia, 125
Bayreuth pit, 143
Béatrice et Bénédict, 130
Beethoven, 12, 139
Belasco, 154
Bel canto era, 28, 101–109, 120, 130
Bellini, Vincenzo, 26, 101
Berg, Alban, 10, 92, 140, 151, 152
Bergonzi, Carlo, 116
Berloiz, 127, 130, 132
Betrothal in a Monastery, 135
Bizet, Georges, 6, 46, 127, 129
Bjoerling, Jussi, 116
Blocking, 42
Boito, Arrigo, 121
Bolcom, William, 164
Bomarzo, 165
Bonynge, Richard, 103, 105